THE BREAKING OF THE BREAD

*An Updated Handbook for
Extraordinary Ministers of Holy Communion*

An Updated Handbook for
Extraordinary Ministers of Holy Communion

The Breaking
of
the Bread

by
Joseph M. Champlin

PAULIST PRESS
New York/Mahwah, N.J.

IMPRIMATUR
Most Reverend Thomas J. Costello, D.D.
Vicar General, Diocese of Syracuse, New York
August 15, 2004

Cover design by Lynn Else; interior art by Ann Dalton
Book design by Theresa M. Sparacio

Library of Congress Cataloging-in-Publication Data

Champlin, Joseph M.
    The breaking of the bread : an updated handbook for extraordinary ministers of Holy Communion / by Joseph M. Champlin.
        p. cm.
    Includes bibliographical references.
    ISBN 0-8091-4314-3 (alk. paper)
    1. Lord's Supper—Lay adminstration—Catholic Church. I. Title.

BX2237.7C43 2005
264'.02036—dc22

                                                                2004020938

Published by Paulist Press
997 Macarthur Boulevard
Mahwah, New Jersey 07430

www.paulistpress.com

Printed and bound in the United States of America

Contents

CONTENTS

Acknowledgments

I wish to thank the many persons who made possible *The Breaking of the Bread: An Updated Handbook for Extraordinary Ministers of Holy Communion.*

- Father Lawrence Boadt, C.S.P., highly regarded scripture scholar and current president of Paulist Press, whose persistent encouragement motivated me to complete this text and a subsequent smaller book on the Eucharist;

- Monsignors James Maroney and Anthony Sherman of the Washington Secretariat for the Bishops' Committee on the Liturgy, for their advice on current official developments;

- The extraordinary ministers of Holy Communion at the Cathedral of the Immaculate Conception in Syracuse, whose personal testimonies begin most of the chapters in this book;

- The people of Holy Cross Parish in Vero Beach, Florida, for their lived example of connecting Sunday

Eucharists and bringing Holy Communion to the sick or homebound;

● The literally thousands of persons for whom the earlier volume, *An Important Office of Immense Love,* served as an introduction and training manual for this sacred ministry;

● Don and Bill, whose testimonies from that previous book have been included in this one;

● Patricia Gale, who has transcribed for nearly a quarter of a century my handwritten manuscripts to computerized printouts and, in this case, had to follow complex directions for combining parts of an older text with something totally new.

Sections of *An Important Office of Immense Love* with substantial editing and updating have been incorporated into *The Breaking of the Bread,* particularly the historical and spirituality portions.

May this new volume be as helpful to today's countless extraordinary ministers of Holy Communion as the earlier text has been for so many in the recent past.

Introduction

Americans in general and Catholics in particular have experienced rapid and radical changes in the past half-century.

Consider a few items then, around fifty years ago, and now, beginning the third millennium.

In the secular world of America—

- Then, homes usually had only one or, at most, a few telephones in them, and people called long distance through an operator. Now, almost everyone carries a cell phone and can reach anywhere by merely punching several numbers.
- Then, people traveling many miles generally took the train. Now, most make long journeys by plane.
- Then, we learned about current events over the radio, through the newspaper, or in newsreels at the local movie theatre. Now, with television we know instantly what is happening around the world and even see the events as they unfold.

In the spiritual world of Catholics—

● Then, Catholics prior to Communion fasted from food and drink after midnight. Now, they abstain from food or drink for only one hour, with water or medicine permissible at any time.

● Then, a full church attended Lenten midday Masses, but only a few hearty souls approached the altar for Communion. Now, in parallel situations, almost everyone moves forward to receive the Eucharist.

● Then, only the priest touched or distributed the consecrated host. Now, thousands of lay men and women, termed extraordinary ministers of Holy Communion, perform that task. For example, at the new and remarkable Our Lady of Angels Cathedral in Los Angeles, more than five hundred persons serve as liturgical ministers, and at Sunday Masses there are over forty Communion stations.

In the late 1970s I wrote *An Important Office of Immense Love: A Handbook for Eucharistic Ministers.* It had a very specific audience and was not designed for the general public. Still, several hundred thousand persons purchased or received the book and even today, a quarter of a century later, a few thousand people yearly obtain copies of it.

Several other authors have produced similar volumes for eucharistic ministers and enjoyed an equally positive response.

The numerical success of these books means that since Pope Paul VI approved the introduction of lay persons as eucharistic ministers in 1973, there has been a veritable explosion in the number of Catholics exercising this function. Such an instant and massive development in the U.S. Catholic Church parallels those rapid and radical changes we have experienced in the secular society of America.

In the spring of 2002, Pope John Paul II published a Third Typical Edition of the *Roman Missal,* including a revised edition of the *General Instruction* as part of that text. It is substantially the same as the First and Second Typical Editions, but contains significant changes based on thirty years of experience with the revised Order of the Mass. In addition, there have been several other authoritative liturgical documents from both the Holy Father in Rome and the American Bishops in Washington that contain items of note for extraordinary ministers of Holy Communion.

Because of these changes, it is time to update my handbook for eucharistic ministers. This update offers a brief historical sketch of eucharistic practice, describes the desired inner qualities of extraordinary ministers, examines two pastoral situations involving the Eucharist, lists a series of often-asked questions with practical responses to each of them and, finally, assembles or summarizes sections in current official directives that impact extraordinary ministers of Holy Communion.

Each chapter will start with a reflection by contemporary individuals on the topic of "How do I feel or have felt while exercising this important office of immense love?"

1

The First Millennium
and Early Middle Ages

I am acutely aware of how experiences being a Cathedral parishioner are interwoven with those of being a eucharistic minister...and it is difficult to separate the two. My husband and I are both Cathedral parishioners and eucharistic ministers. It is most evident to me that the combined experience has had an extremely positive impact on our forty-year marriage... we think of Sunday evening Mass almost as a "date"...and indeed, often ask friends to join us for the service and dinner afterward because of our desire to share the uplifting experience. We look forward to the weeks that we are assigned to assume eucharistic minister responsibilities...and are eager to "fill in" when needed on unassigned weeks. The whole experience has brought my husband and me closer...to each other...to our Church...and to our God.

In addition, after being a Catholic for almost forty years, I am somewhat reluctant to admit that I am now much more aware of, and attentive to, the different parts of the Mass. I have a brand new perspective on the Mass since becoming a eucharistic minister and feel as though I get so much more out of it than I ever did before.

Being a eucharistic minister has made me feel extremely blessed as I am allowed to distribute the Blood and Body of Christ. With those blessings, however, comes a real worry that I am not worthy of this holy task. Also comes a worry that I cannot connect enough with each recipient to instill in him or her the same overwhelming sense of holiness that I experience when the priest presents the Precious Body to me. I try hard to look in each person's eyes and touch his or her hand as I place the wafer in his or her palm...and pray that my contact has helped to make the experience more meaningful for the receiver. I try not to let my words become "ho-hum," and want every recipient to feel unique and special. This responsibility is burdensome, yet awesome...and one which I treasure.

—Janice

The introduction thirty years ago of extraordinary ministers of Holy Communion exemplified another new, yet old, procedure being restored to meet the liturgical needs of our day. Our brief historical overview should make that clear.

Jesuit Father Joseph Jungmann's massive volume, *The Mass of the Roman Rite,* has long been judged our most comprehensive and accurate history of the liturgy. In that text he describes the various procedures for receiving Communion that have been customary over the twenty centuries of Catholic tradition.[1]

Up until the fourth century it was a rule, not merely an ideal, that the faithful communicate at every Mass. Believers understood clearly that the action of all receiving the Lord's Body and Blood formed an integral and natural part of every eucharistic celebration. Nevertheless, priests normally celebrated only on Sundays.

As a consequence, the faithful both communicated at that Sabbath Eucharist and took a sufficient supply of sacred particles home with them for the week ahead. There these early believers carefully preserved the consecrated bread, consumed a portion of it day after day before eating their regular food, and gave a particle to others.

This practice of lay persons—or, more specifically here, those not priests or deacons—keeping the sacred particles within the home also made it possible for the sick, prisoners, and isolated monks to communicate frequently, even daily, despite the fact that weekday Mass was then a rarity.

It is evident from historical research that lay persons ordinarily received the Lord directly into their hands for the first nine centuries. Writings, pictures, and documentation speak of or illustrate this practice.

ST. CYRIL, BISHOP OF JERUSALEM

The most widely quoted proof of this assertion is an instruction that St. Cyril, the bishop of Jerusalem, issued on the Sunday after Easter in 348. Speaking to a group of adults received into the Church just a few days earlier, he outlined the proper method for receiving our Lord in Communion.

> When you approach (Communion) do not come with your hands outstretched or with your fingers open, but make your left hand a throne for the right one, which is to receive the King. With your hand hollowed receive the body of Christ and answer Amen. After having, with every precaution, sanctified your eyes by

7

contact with the holy body, consume it, making sure that not a particle is wasted, for that would be like losing one of your own limbs. Tell me, if you were given some gold dust, would you not hold it very carefully for fear of letting any of it fall and losing it? How much more careful, then, you should be not to let fall even a crumb of something more precious than gold or jewels! After receiving the body of Christ, approach the chalice of his Blood. Do not stretch out your hands, but bow in an attitude of adoration and reverence, and say Amen (*Mystagogic Catechesis* V, 21, 1–22, 4).[2]

St. Theodore of Mopsuestia (d. 428) offered this commentary: "Everyone stretches out his right hand to receive the Eucharist, which is given, and puts his left hand under it."

A century or so after that, St. John of Damascus (d. 570) observed: "Making the figure of the cross with our hands, we receive the body of Christ crucified."

Finally, even as late as the ninth century, a sacramentary, or altar book, contained a Communion scene showing the Eucharist placed in the hand of the communicant.

The practice, thus, of lay persons touching, holding, and distributing the consecrated bread has deep roots in our Catholic past. In fact, we can maintain with good backing that such activities were more common than not throughout the first eight or nine centuries of the Church.

CHANGE: MIDDLE AGES

For very complex reasons the pattern then changed, and handling or distributing the Eucharist became a practice more and more reserved to the clergy alone. Was this shift mainly a result of abuses, of sacrilegious or irreverent use of the consecrated particles by lay communicants or distributors?

Some contemporary critics who opposed the restoration of Communion in the hand or the reestablishment of lay ministers for the Eucharist argued that this was the case. However, the historical data does not seem to support that objection. There were clearly occasional abuses, and an official decision or two addressed those situations. But other testimonies in the Middle Ages reveal various irreverent incidents even when Communion was placed directly on the tongue.

The more substantive causes behind the change that restricted distributors to clerics alone appear to be different developing attitudes about the Eucharist itself and our liturgical worship.

In those medieval days many Christians began to emphasize the divine aspects of the Eucharist and to stress the real, holy, tremendous, awesome presence of Christ our God in the sacrament. The host was, in a way, to be adored more than to be eaten. Our unworthiness in the face of this sublime gift led to less-frequent reception of Communion, a greater distance between altar and pew, and more cautions surrounding the celebration of Mass.

Concurrently in those centuries the laity were gradually eliminated from the liturgy, even from "sacred places" like the altar, which became reserved territories for clerics and in some cases for priests alone.

In fact, during the eighth and ninth centuries, lay persons were almost totally excluded from public worship. The priest alone stood at the altar and at an ever-increasing distance from the congregation; the laity no longer brought offerings to the altar within the Mass, but were required to do so beforehand; singing was done by a special schola or small choir only; the general intercessions disappeared; the faithful now could not see what was happening on the altar because the celebrant blocked their view; the canon or eucharistic prayer was said quietly; and everything took place in silence or in a language less-understood by the people.

For older Catholics all of that sounds quite familiar and should remind them of the Church they grew up in and which held sway as late as the 1950s and 1960s.

This brief historical overview, although simplified and thus necessarily incomplete, nevertheless provides us with a background of understanding behind many popular traditions or principles in pre-Vatican II Catholicism:

"The wedding Mass is one of the rare occasions you as a lay person are allowed in the sanctuary." "Never chew the host." "One should always be silent in God's house." "Make sure you go to confession before going to Communion."

These notions grew out of a frame of reference that developed at the end of the first millennium and differed in many ways from the approaches of the first centuries of Catholicism. Those medieval concepts obviously were handed down very carefully to us by our forefathers of the faith. They had value, respected one aspect of the mystery that is the Eucharist, and should not be casually disregarded.

In the next chapter we will trace some of the movements or steps—official and unofficial, from both below and above—which have reversed, as it were, the process. These grassroots efforts and authoritative Roman documents gave theological bases and practical impetus for restoring the laity's part in liturgy. Extraordinary ministers of Holy Communion, including lay men and women, were a natural outgrowth of that trend as well as a pragmatic solution to a pastoral problem.

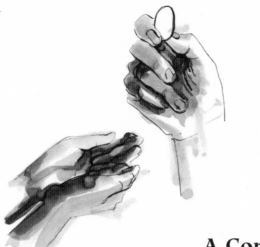

A Contemporary
Shift Backward and Forward

My first experience of distributing Communion truly was a chilling one. I remember when I put my name on the list at the Mass when you asked for volunteers. Then I received a schedule and, lo and behold, there was my name. Yikes—a whole gamut of emotions began, starting with the feeling of unworthiness. All the "What if's," "Should I's," and "Can I's" went through my head up until the first night.

It was a 5:10 Mass, and my husband was unable to attend with me, which made it harder. I went to you to confession beforehand and told you I was a bit apprehensive. You gave your usual uplifting support.

I didn't expect the feeling that happened that night. I picked up the host with trembling hands, looked up, and there was a man standing there with a kind and happy smile. It wasn't the usual smile a stranger gives in passing, but it was an expression I read as his happiness to receive God. My head immediately got this big chill; you know, the kind that you need to put your hands on top of your head. It was a wonderful and lasting chill. I continued with a tear in my eye and I saw many more of these same expressions, happy, reverent faces. (A few not too happy I might add, actually a few downright nasty-looking.)

It was years later that I first distributed to my husband. I had my head down to pick up the host, and then I looked up and there he was. Well, I just filled with tears and I couldn't talk. It's a feeling that is hard to explain, but trust me when I say it's a great feeling. He told me he also had his own feelings not describable. He paused a minute so I could get myself back together for the next.

Being a eucharistic minister truly has made a powerful impact on my life, and for that I thank you for giving me the opportunity. I think we all become a bit jaded, for lack of a better word, and just go through the motions. I think we all do it when something becomes routine, but how lucky am I to say that God is part of my routine. I could go on and on but speaking of routines, I must get back to work before they take this routine away.

—Kay

At the end of the nineteenth century, several European monasteries began to look at their liturgies and ask questions. Common sense, loving concern, and historical research indicated that the then-current style of worship left something to be desired. The monks at Solesmes, Beuron, Maria Laach, and Louvain, among others, consequently attempted to discover and recover some of the better liturgical practices of the past.[1]

The reforms that they encouraged naturally had a monastic orientation, but at Klosterneuberg in Austria, Father Pius Parsch sought to apply the fruit of this new thinking and ancient research into parish life. His pastoral efforts were to be the inspiration for many similar labors in Europe and the United States, including those of Monsignor Martin B. Hellriegel at Holy Cross Church in St. Louis, Missouri.

Such grassroots suggestions soon received papal approval and support. St. Pius X in 1903 issued a decree on sacred music that called for reforms in that sphere, and also urged involvement of lay persons in the sacred liturgy.

In a classic, pivotal, oft-quoted statement, this Holy Father declared that the "most important and indispensable source" of "the true Christian spirit" is the faithful's "active participation in the most sacred mysteries and in the public and solemn prayer of the Church."[2] That ushered in, officially, a totally new trend: restoring the faithful, the laity, to their rightful place in worship and calling upon all present to be active participants.

The first half of our century witnessed a constant interplay between a push from below for further reforms in the liturgy and a prod from above that changed various rituals.

Catholics began to receive Communion at an earlier age and were encouraged by papal directives to approach the sacred table frequently, even daily.

Liturgical reformers pleaded for what some termed revolutionary, even heretical innovations: an altar facing the people, vernacular liturgies, lay persons reading the scriptures, Holy Week services at hours more in conformity with their original times. The proponents often faced opposition, rejection, or ridicule.

THE MYSTICAL BODY OF CHRIST

Then, in 1943, Pope Pius XII issued the encyclical *On the Mystical Body of Christ* that came to serve as the theological basis for various liturgical reforms. It spoke of the Church as the mystical body of the Lord and thereby highlighted the dignity of each member.

To that effect, Pius cited words of St. Leo uttered centuries earlier: "Recognize, O Christian, your dignity, and being made a sharer of the divine nature go not back to your former worthlessness along the way of unseemly conduct. Keep in mind of what Head and of what body you are a member."[3]

Membership in this Church not only gives each Christian a unique dignity, it also binds us together with one another. Pope Pius viewed the Mass as giving special evidence "of our union among ourselves and with our divine Head, marvelous as it is and beyond all praise."[4]

That dignity and closeness, that rightful place of lay persons in worship, nevertheless, does not in any way diminish the singular position of the priest or his importance for the liturgy. "In this act of sacrifice, through the hands of the priest, whose word alone has brought the immaculate Lamb to be present on the altar, the faithful themselves with one desire and one prayer offer it to the eternal Father...."[5]

MEDIATOR DEI

Dignity, participation, bond with one another, community, priesthood: these concepts were taken up in detail a few years later, in 1947, by the same pontiff in his encyclical letter *Mediator Dei* (On the Sacred Liturgy).

14

The following excerpt has particular relevance for any person who has been appointed as an extraordinary minister of Holy Communion: "By the waters of baptism, as by common right, Christians are made members of the mystical body of Christ the Priest, and by the 'character' which is imprinted on their souls they are appointed to give worship to God; thus they participate, according to their condition, in the priesthood of Christ."[6]

The many and varied changes introduced by the Church in the post-World War II years and prior to the Second Vatican Council in one way or another simply flow from these fundamental notions.

For example, a mitigation of the eucharistic fast rules removed obstacles that in modern times had kept the laity from Communion. Introduction of the vernacular promoted participation by the congregation in word and song. Reversal of altars brought priest and people closer together as a family, a community, a mystical body in worship.

VATICAN II: LITURGICAL REFORM

On December 4, 1963, these scattered half-century of official and unofficial reform movements were tied together by publication of the *Constitution on the Sacred Liturgy*.

The Council Fathers understandably brought out once more those key notions of the lay person's participation and dignity: "Mother Church earnestly desires that all the faithful should be led to that full, conscious and active participation in liturgical celebrations which is demanded by the very nature of the liturgy. Such participation by the Christian people as 'a chosen race, a royal priesthood, a holy nation, a redeemed people' (1 Pet 2:9, see 2:4–5), is their right and duty by reason of their baptism."[7]

They likewise underscored the community nature of liturgy: "It is to be stressed that whenever rites, according to their specific nature, make provision for communal celebration involving the presence and active participation of the faithful, this way of celebrating them is to be preferred, so far as possible, to a celebration that is individual and quasi-private."[8]

Finally, the Vatican Council document once and for all indicated that not only the priest but also others have a true function to perform. A totally clerical liturgy should be an experience of the past: "In liturgical celebrations each person, minister or layman, who has an office to perform should do all of, but only, those parts which pertain to his office by the nature of the rite and the principles of liturgy."[9]

The revised ritual books published after the Council—for Mass, the sacraments, the Church year, the Liturgy of the Hours—faithfully follow the principles of reform enunciated in the *Constitution on the Sacred Liturgy*. The Order of Mass, to illustrate, makes provision for Communion under both kinds.

Nevertheless, there was no explicit mention made in that Constitution or in the Order of Mass for extraordinary ministers of Holy Communion. However, as the number of communicants multiplied because of the reforms noted above, and as the availability of priests, deacons, or acolytes diminished because of deaths or resignations, the need for such persons developed.

DOCUMENTS ISSUED BY PAUL VI

On January 29, 1973, Pope Paul VI issued the instruction *Immensae Caritatis* (Facilitating Sacramental Communion in Particular Circumstances).[10] In that document the Holy Father said: "First of all, provision must be made lest reception of Communion become impossible or difficult because of insufficient ministers."

Paul VI envisioned two situations in which such a lack of adequate personnel could exist: either during or outside Mass. The commentary by the United States Bishops' Committee on the Liturgy spells these circumstances in detail:

a. when there is a large number of regular communicants at the parochial liturgy and a shortage of ordinary ministers to assist the president of the assembly in the distribution of the Eucharist. A shortage of eucharistic ministers, in such a case, causes the Communion rite to be out of proportion to the total celebration. The goal is not, however, to shorten or have more efficient Masses, but to give them their proper value and to avoid the rush it takes to distribute Communion to everyone present.

b. when outside Mass the ordinary minister is impeded from fulfilling his office due to age, bad health, or other pastoral demands.

c. when there is a shortage of ordinary ministers of the Eucharist (e.g., in some mission countries where the catechist has traditionally led the Sunday prayer service when no priest, deacon, or acolyte was present).[11]

Several months later the Holy See published a section of the Roman Ritual entitled *Holy Communion and Worship of the Eucharist Outside of Mass*. It reflected the development and official approval of ministers for Holy Communion by providing rituals "if the minister is not a priest or deacon" and for "administration of Communion and Viaticum to the sick by an extraordinary minister."[12]

In his instruction endorsing extraordinary ministers, Pope Paul VI described the Eucharist as a testament of Christ's "immense love," a "wonderful gift," and "the greatest gift of all," and he insisted that "the greatest reverence toward this sacrament be constantly maintained."[13] We thus can never display adequate reverence for Holy Communion nor bring to the altar appropriate holiness.

However, from the perspective outlined in this chapter, a Catholic lay person or religious who has received the sacraments of initiation—baptism, confirmation, and the Eucharist—does have the fundamental dignity or worthiness to serve in that function. Moreover, the Church in its authoritative decrees has been calling for greater participation in the liturgy, more distribution of roles, and, now, even appointment of the laity as extraordinary ministers of Holy Communion. Finally, in a parish or worshiping community, the leadership people may judge that it needs these ministers, and will carefully select suitable candidates and then publicly commission these persons.

Nevertheless, the notion of "Lord, I am not worthy" frequently appears in the testimony of new, or even veteran, extraordinary ministers of the Eucharist. In a certain sense, no one is really worthy of this task. But neither is any person worthy to serve as a deacon, priest, bishop, or pope.

Still, both ordinary and extraordinary ministers of Holy Communion need to cultivate certain inner and exterior qualities to become as worthy as possible while fulfilling their sacred tasks. We will now discuss some of those qualities.

Called to Holiness I:
Weak but Strong Persons of Faith

About twenty-five years ago as an altar boy, I had a very different view of Jesus Christ in the Holy Eucharist. He was a white wafer, large or small. The large one was inscribed with IHS, and, on occasions such as Benediction, was enshrined in a golden monstrance for all to adore as the priest elevated it in a cloud of incense. The small hosts were distributed to the faithful at Communion.

This was the sacrament that could only be touched by the priest; you couldn't even reach in to dislodge it from the roof of your mouth where it invariably became stuck. "Don't chew it; don't touch it; it is sacred; we have gold plates to catch it if it falls and the consecrated hands of the priest to administer it or to retrieve it." God was kept in a gold tabernacle and the wafers were made only by nuns. I always felt quite unworthy to receive the Lord in Communion, and the laws governing the sacrament made it all the more removed from me.

Over the past several years, great changes in the sacrament have made Jesus a closer friend. A more relaxed and personal relationship has been formed between us. Jesus used earthen dishes when he consecrated the bread and wine of the Last Supper into his Body and Blood, not golden cups and platters. He was dealing with common men and he too was a common man. Now he is again reachable and has been brought back to humanness by a Church that feels for its people. With the advent of bread baked by lay people, Communion in the hand, and a relaxation of the fasting rules, I believe that Jesus Christ has been put back into our lives on a more personal level than ever before.

To be asked to be a minister of Communion caused me a great deal of consternation. I felt like the altar boy of twenty-five years ago, unworthy to touch the Body of Christ, unable to feel a personal relationship to the Holy Eucharist because it was still a very sacred object. At the same time there was an excitement about being put into the position to become more than I had ever been before, to be one of only a few who were thought worthy enough to be a minister of Communion. I was really put into a tough position. All that I had ever been taught about the sacrament from the time I was eight and a novice altar server was on one side telling me no and the new more personal, more loving Church that I know today was saying that it was acceptable. I felt that I could at least give it a try.

I am very happy now that I decided to try. I feel closer to Jesus Christ and the sacrament of Communion than I ever have before. I feel that I have experienced a change in my attitude toward others and a perceptible change in my own lifestyle. Being on the altar on Sunday and distributing Communion to my family and friends makes me want to be more, to be someone whom people can trust and look up to, and to do what is right, not just what is convenient or easy. I want to be closer to Jesus through my ministry and closer to others because of it.

—*Bill*

The desire for self-improvement and holiness that accompanies functioning as an extraordinary minister of the Eucharist obviously deserves support and praise. It also reflects sentiments of the Second Vatican Council addressed to priests, but which apply with equal force to Communion distributors.

> Priestly holiness itself contributes very greatly to a fruitful fulfillment of the priestly ministry. True, the grace of God can complete the work of salvation even through unworthy ministers. Yet ordinarily God desires to manifest his wonders through those who have been made particularly docile to the impulse and guidance of the Holy Spirit. Because of their intimate union with Christ and their holiness of life, these men can say with the apostle: "It is no longer I that live, but Christ lives in me." (Gal 2:20)[1]

Persons who espouse such idealism, but struggle with human frailty, can nevertheless take comfort in the example of Jesus and the words of Scripture.

Our Lord selected persons whose faults have been highlighted in the Bible. Impetuous Peter boasted of his loyalty, then almost immediately under pressure denied his Master. The skeptic Thomas boldly asserted he would not believe unless he probed Christ's nail-prints and put his hands into Jesus' side. James and John, along with Peter, were asked by the Master to support him in Gethsemane when he felt deep sorrow, fear, and distress. Instead, they fell asleep. "So you could not keep watch with me for one hour?"[2]

21

The Lord's response to their drowsiness is really meant for all of us. "Watch and pray that you may not undergo the test. The spirit is willing, but the flesh is weak."[3]

The power of God's grace transformed these weak individuals, carrying them on to great sanctity and to the ultimate self-giving of martyrdom.

St. Paul speaks in similar fashion about human weakness and amazing grace. A thorn in the flesh, an angel of Satan, continually attacked this apostle to keep him from pride.

> Three times I begged the Lord about this, that it might leave me, but he said to me, "My grace is sufficient for you, for power is made perfect in weakness." I will rather boast most gladly of my weaknesses, in order that the power of Christ may dwell with me. Therefore I am content with weakness, insults, hardships, persecutions, and constraints for the sake of Christ; for when I am weak, then I am strong.[4]

The grace of God, then, will be sufficient for ministers of Communion as it has and will be for others like Paul. Its end product is both a reform of personal habits or a transformation of lifestyle and the development of certain desirable inner qualities.

Dr. Elisabeth Kübler-Ross, whose writings on death and dying are world-known, observed once how important are the interior attitudes of clergy who visit the terminally ill. Their faith, or lack of it, will be detected by the deathly sick, sometimes without a word being spoken, and thus either encourage or discourage those hurting patients. In extraordinary ministers of Holy Communion the positive interior qualities or their regrettable absence will likewise be evident to others in the worshiping community.

These dispositions, too, will thus build up or tear down the Body of Christ.

FAITH

Inner faith is, of course, the essential foundation for all Catholic worship. Unless the interior eye passes through the external signs and symbols of our liturgies; unless it looks beyond the words, actions, and materials of our public prayer to a deeper reality present; unless it sees something beneath our sacramental rituals—then we are a deceived people practicing hollow, artificial, even magical ceremonies.

Faith enables us to pass through, look beyond, and see beneath the outer shell. Through faith we recognize the presence of Christ in various ways within our liturgies.

Those many presences of the Lord, originally outlined so clearly in paragraph 7 of Vatican II's *Constitution on the Sacred Liturgy,* are nicely summarized in the introduction to the ritual for *Holy Communion Outside of Mass:*

> In the celebration of Mass the chief ways in which Christ is present in his Church gradually become clear. First he is present in the very assembly of the faithful, gathered together in his name; next he is present in his word, when the Scriptures are read in the Church and explained; then in the person of the minister; finally and above all, in the eucharistic sacrament. In a way that is completely unique, the whole and entire Christ, God and man, is substantially and permanently present in the sacrament. This presence of Christ under the appearance of bread and wine "is called real, not to exclude other kinds of presence as if they were not real, but because it is real par excellence."[5]

An awareness of those presences and faith in them will affect the way a minister of Communion fulfills her or his function. That personal faith will overflow into one's attitudes and actions.

A change takes place within us when we become conscious that Jesus dwells in our midst as we pray together. We listen more attentively and prepare more carefully when we reflect that it is the Lord who speaks in the scriptures. We touch, consume, and handle more reverently the consecrated species when we fully appreciate that it is truly Christ's Body and Blood beneath the bread and wine.

Faith in this real eucharistic presence is the most critical quality for a minister of Communion. To believe that "the Holy Eucharist contains the entire spiritual treasure of the Church, that is, Christ himself, our Passover and living bread";[6] to believe that "Christ the Lord is offered in the Sacrifice of the Mass when he becomes present sacramentally as the spiritual food of the faithful under the appearance of bread and wine";[7] to believe that "after the sacrifice has been offered...as long as the Eucharist is reserved in churches and oratories, Christ is truly Emmanuel, that is, 'God with us'";[8] to believe that "he is in our midst day and night; full of grace and truth, he dwells among us"[9]—to believe these truths of the Church in the depths of our hearts constitutes the "need of only one thing" by the Lord for a suitable distributor of the Eucharist.[10]

That faith, however, is not a static quality. It can grow and, alas, may weaken and even be lost. For that reason "[Christians] gather at Mass that we may hear and express our faith again in this assembly and, by expressing it, renew and deepen it."[11]

"People in love make signs of love, not only to express their love but also to deepen it. Love never expressed dies. Christians' love for Christ and for one another and Christians' faith in Christ and in one another, must be expressed in the signs and symbols of celebration or they will die."[12]

Or put another way, "[F]aith grows when it is well expressed in celebration. Good celebrations foster and nourish faith. Poor celebrations weaken and destroy faith."[13]

The minister of Holy Communion, then, like the priest or deacon, can foster and nourish or weaken and destroy faith. That distributor's own inner faith is the key factor here. The following words of our American bishops about the priest celebrant apply as well to the minister of Communion.

"No other single factor affects the liturgy as much as the attitude, style, and bearing of the celebrant: his sincere faith and warmth as he welcomes the worshiping community; his human naturalness combined with dignity and seriousness as he breaks the Bread of Word and Eucharist."[14]

A great opportunity, a great challenge, a great responsibility.

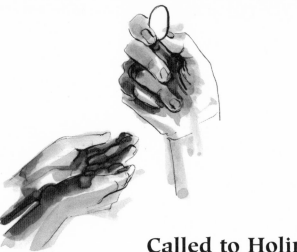

4

Called to Holiness II:
Prayerful, Adoring,
Joyful Ministers

PRAYERFULNESS

Out of faith develops an attitude of prayerfulness. We stand before God in a spirit of awe, reverence, and dependence.

When Moses came to Horeb, the mountain of God, an angel of the Lord appeared to him out of a bush which, though on fire, was not consumed. As Moses moved over more closely to examine this remarkable phenomenon, "God said: 'Come no nearer! Remove the sandals from your feet, for the place where you stand is holy ground. I am the God of your father,' he continued, 'the God of Abraham, the God of Isaac, the God of Jacob.' Moses hid his face, for he was afraid to look at God."[1]

An attitude of "remove your sandals and hide your face" awe before our transcendent, majestic Lord will come across to people. Such an inner spirit of reverence and prayerfulness is transparent. People sense and recognize it, just as they intuit and detect its absence.

Such an attitude will affect the way we walk about the sanctuary, fold our hands, genuflect, distribute the host, and hand over the cup. There should be no casualness, no rush. Rather, there should be careful, deliberate gestures, although natural and honest ones.

Dealing the eucharistic bread to others as if this were a fast card game and placing it on the hand or tongue before a communicant can whisper "Amen" are bad habits caused rather easily by routine, but they communicate to others a lack of prayerfulness in the minister.

ADORATION

Closely akin to that spirit of prayer is the stance of adoration. The Church insists that "all the faithful show this holy sacrament the veneration and adoration which is due to God himself....Nor is the sacrament to be less the object of adoration because it was instituted by Christ the Lord to be received as food."[2]

That sense of adoration expresses itself often during the eucharistic liturgy. For example, in the Gloria of the Mass the congregation shouts, as it were, "We worship you, we give you thanks, we praise you for your glory." The people's response to the Preface, as another illustration, reflects an Old Testament angelic hymn of adoration: "Holy, holy, holy Lord, God of power and might...."

A spirit of prayerful adoration should permeate ministers throughout the celebration of Mass and during the distribution of Holy Communion. But it also ought to bring them frequently to the tabernacle for private, personal meditation outside of Mass. Prayer before the Lord reserved in that location finds its origin in the Mass and leads people back to the eucharistic sacrifice itself. Logically speaking, those with the greatest devotion to the Mass will at the same time have an intense relationship with Christ the Lord in the tabernacle; conversely, the person who prays regularly before the reserved sacrament should possess a deep love for holy Mass.

Forms of Worship of the Eucharist (part of the larger Roman document *Holy Communion and Worship of the Eucharist Outside of Mass*) addresses this matter at length:

> When the faithful honor Christ present in the sacrament, they should remember that this presence is derived from the sacrifice and is directed toward sacramental and spiritual Communion.
>
> The same piety which moves the faithful to eucharistic adoration attracts them to a deeper participation in the paschal mystery. It makes them respond gratefully to the gifts of Christ who by his humanity continues to pour divine life upon the members of his body. Living with Christ the Lord, they achieve a close familiarity with him and in his presence pour out their hearts for themselves and for those dear to them; they pray for peace and for the salvation of the world. Offering their entire lives with Christ to the Father in the Holy Spirit, they draw from this wondrous exchange an increase of faith, hope and love. Thus they nourish the proper disposition to celebrate the memorial of the Lord as devoutly as possible and to receive frequently the bread given to us by the Father.
>
> The faithful should make every effort to worship Christ the Lord in the sacrament, depending upon the

circumstances of their own life. Pastors should encourage them in this by example and word.

Prayer before Christ the Lord sacramentally present extends the union with Christ which the faithful have reached in Communion. It renews the covenant which in turn moves them to maintain in their lives what they have received by faith and by sacraments. They should try to lead their whole lives with the strength derived from the heavenly food, as they share in the depth and resurrection of the Lord. Everyone should be concerned with good deeds and with pleasing God so that he or she may imbue the world with the Christian spirit and be a witness of Christ in the midst of human society.[3]

After the faithful and the minister have participated in the Eucharist, the Church recommends that each one who has been refreshed by Communion should remain in prayer for a period of time. That prayerful personal thanksgiving simply continues what the Mass itself does so perfectly—giving thanks to the Father through Christ and in the Spirit.[4]

Leaving the altar and the church does not mean abandoning the presence of Christ there or removing his influence on our daily work and world. "The union with Christ, to which the sacrament is directed, should be extended to the whole of Christian life. Thus the faithful, constantly reflecting upon the gift they have received, should carry on their daily work with thanksgiving, under the guidance of the Holy Spirit, and should bring forth fruits of rich charity."[5]

The rubrics for Mass mention that a priest at the Eucharist "should serve God and the people with dignity and humility, and by his bearing and by the way he says the divine words he must convey to the faithful the living presence of Christ."[6]

With adaptations, that exhortation applies to ministers of Holy Communion who must serve with dignity and humility, impressing upon others the living presence of God. Only a prayerful person can do that.

JOY

The presence of Jesus brought joy to people's hearts.

At the first Christmas, an angel reassured frightened shepherds with these words: "Do not be afraid; for behold, I proclaim to you good news of great joy that will be for all the people."[7]

After his death, the risen Lord appeared to the eleven and said, "Touch me." He showed them his hands and his feet, but they were "still incredulous for joy and were amazed" over his presence in their midst.[8]

Following Pentecost, the first Christians lived a communal life. "Every day they devoted themselves to meeting together in the temple area and to breaking bread in their homes. They ate their meals with exultation and sincerity of heart, praising God and enjoying favor with all the people."[9] There are fairly good reasons for arguing that this paragraph from the Acts of the Apostles includes an indirect reference to the Eucharist. In any event, their inner selves experienced great joy during those days together as they broke bread.

St. Paul, writing to the early believers of Galatia, taught that the fruit of the spirit is love, joy, peace, patient endurance, kindness, generosity, faith, mildness, and chastity.[10] To the Thessalonians, he simply gave this directive: "Rejoice always."[11]

The minister of Communion should experience and radiate some of that joy. He or she has indeed heard the tidings of great joy, touched the risen Jesus' body, broken bread with others at the Lord's table, received the Holy Spirit in baptism and confirmation, and accepted the mandate or encouragement of Paul to rejoice always.

Those inner qualities of peace, love, and joy will, like faith, adoration, and prayerfulness, be evident to other parishioners. Persons with such transparent joy naturally attract others to themselves and win these people over. Their own joy is contagious; it spreads; it quietly seeps into a neighbor's being and begins to lift up that individual's spirit; it is shared without any loss to the sharer.

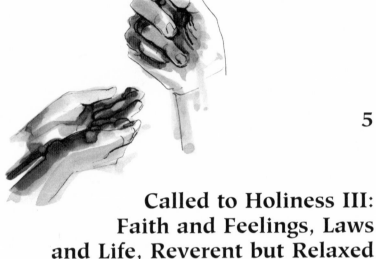

Called to Holiness III:
Faith and Feelings, Laws
and Life, Reverent but Relaxed

FAITH AND FEELINGS:
SPIRITUAL JOY AND FLUCTUATING EMOTIONS

Eucharistic ministers, like all those with special ministerial functions or even like every believer for that matter, need to beware of confusing or identifying spiritual joy with pure feelings of elation. They may be the same at times, but not always, or necessarily.

We can experience a profound inner serenity and yet feel blue, bad, or bored. On the other hand, an individual may feel "sky high" or wildly excited and still lack deep peace and joy.

The problems that accompany routine affect every area of life, including such sacred and sublime activities as offering Mass or distributing the Eucharist. We may feel no enthusiasm, seem to take the privilege for granted, and wonder if our faith has grown weak or our reverence for the sacrament has diminished.

The emotional zeal of a newly ordained priest or a freshly installed minister of Holy Communion does not last forever. No one lives a life of peaks and plateaus alone; there are valleys of darkness and low moments for all.

A faith-filled celebration may be feelingless; a feeling-filled liturgy could be faithless.

Our American bishops summarized this rather well:

> Celebrations need not fail, even on a particular Sunday when our feelings do not match the invitation of Christ and his Church to worship. Faith does not always permeate our failings. But the sign and symbols of worship can give bodily expression to faith as we celebrate. Our own faith is stimulated. We become one with others whose faith is similarly expressed. We rise above our own feelings to respond to God in prayer.[1]

Practically speaking, this means performing our task with faith, prayerfulness, and care regardless of the current mood or feeling. The spirit of Christian joy and peace within us will still shine through despite what our emotions may seem to tell us at that moment.

SAVED, BUT STILL WEAK AND SINFUL SERVANTS

I saw a bumper sticker recently that announced: "Christians are not saints, just saved."

That motto carries considerable wisdom with it. The basic reason for our inner joy is a realization that we have been forgiven by the Blood of Christ, that salvation is possible for us because of the Lord's coming, dying, and rising. God calls us to believe in the Savior and to mirror Jesus' life in our own. But we are saved by grace, not merely by our own works.

A realization of this can bring great peace and deep joy in the midst of our weaknesses and failures. In earlier paragraphs we have outlined the call for holiness and the model Christian behavior expected in a eucharistic minister. Those ideals remain intact. But what of lapses, sins, and mistakes? These certainly cause sadness within. Should they likewise keep us from our ministry at the altar?

The Church deals with that situation in some detail when it discusses the dispositions needed for Communion and, consequently, for a eucharistic minister.

> The Eucharist continuously makes present among men the paschal mystery of Christ. It is the source of every grace and of the forgiveness of sins. Nevertheless, those who intend to receive the body of the Lord must approach it with a pure conscience and proper dispositions of soul if they are to receive the effects of the paschal sacrament.
>
> On this account the Church prescribes "that no one conscious of mortal sin, even though he seems to be contrite, may go to the Holy Eucharist without previous sacramental confession." In urgent necessity and if no confessor is available, he should simply make an act of perfect contrition with the intention of confessing individually, at the proper time, the mortal sins which he cannot confess at present.
>
> It is desirable that those who receive Communion daily or very often go to the sacrament of penance at regular intervals, depending on their circumstances.
>
> Besides this, the faithful should look upon the Eucharist as an antidote which frees them from daily

faults and keeps them from mortal sins; they should also understand the proper way to use the penitential parts of the liturgy, especially at Mass.[2]

Part of that cleansing, disposition-building process involves fasting from food and drink beforehand. As a sort of review for ministers of the Eucharist, we summarize the current legislation found in the 1983 code of Canon Law.

• *Before receiving the Most Holy Eucharist we are to abstain at least one hour from any food or drink, except for only water and medicine.*

Note that this is one hour *before Communion,* not before Mass. Also observe that this Canon 919 states "at least" one hour before Communion, implying the desirability of fasting even for a longer period of time, such as from the midnight fast prior to the change in 1964.

The custom of fasting before Communion arose in the third century and became an obligation imposed by early church councils. Such fasting was and is seen as a spiritual preparation for the Eucharist and a method of showing reverence for this Most Blessed Sacrament.

When church choirs rehearse and religion classes meet prior to Mass, often having refreshments during this time, a reminder of the one-hour fast might be both necessary and instructive.

• *The elderly or infirm and those who care for them may receive the Most Holy Eucharist even if they have eaten something within the prescribed hour.*

This represents a change from previous legislation that required a fifteen-minute period of fasting for those sick in hospitals or at home, for those homebound due to old age, or for persons living in nursing homes.[3]

LAWS AND LIFE, REVERENT BUT RELAXED

It is difficult to be joyful or to radiate joy when we feel uptight or are preoccupied with rubrical rules and regulations. Our attention then focuses on the external deed or word and loses sight of the divine reality beneath and beyond those signs or symbols.

Personal testimonies often mention inner nervousness, worried concern, shaking hands, or moist palms as these people prepared for or discharged their ministry. A bit of that could be traced to the newness of this task and the understandable desire to perform it properly. But much of that anxiety may grow out of an excessive attention to the right procedure and undue concentration on suitable reverence.

Here is a thumb rule for eucharistic ministers, an overall approach or attitude: "Be reverent, but relaxed; comfortable, but not casual."

The Church always urges a balanced view, a middle road in doctrinal teaching and pastoral practice. The principle we have just enunciated fits into that category.

Our bishops in the United States have only these words about the proper decorum for a eucharistic distributor. "It is of the greatest importance that the minister avoid all rush and haste. His [or her] ministration of Communion should be done with dignity and reverence."[4]

Dignity and reverence. No rush or haste. Careful. Relaxed. At ease. Natural. Oneself.

After all, the Mass, as well as other forms of liturgy, is a celebration. The initial chapter of the *General Instruction* for the Order of Mass carries the title, "Importance and Dignity of the Eucharistic Celebration." That brief section alone uses the term "celebration" many times.[5] A celebration, however described or defined, implies a relaxed, easy, joyful event.

The Eucharist, moreover, is a paschal meal or sacred banquet in which participants eat and drink. Only on the most formal of circumstances, the very first occasion with a family, or the initial dinner out with a date do we feel uptight and anxious while eating. Even in those circumstances, that tension should and generally does ease after the beginning moments. It ought to be the same with us during Communion.

The Communion song at Mass is meant to express the spiritual union of communicants who join their voices in singing, to reflect the joy of all, and to make the procession itself a reflection of and a means to build oneness among all participants.[6]

Such spiritual union, joy, and oneness presume that the participants, including the extraordinary ministers of Holy Communion, are relaxed while still reverent, comfortable and at ease, even though not casual or careless.

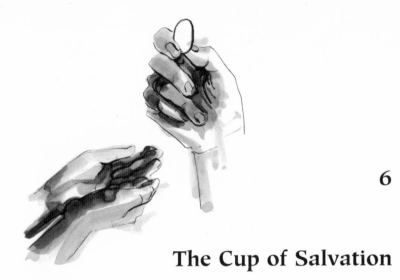

The Cup of Salvation

I was surprised at my selection to be a minister of Communion, and although the option to refuse was available, I knew I would not decline. I felt that I was being called not by man but by God to perform a small but important duty previously reserved for the priest. It was a special privilege for me since I was always taught that the host was to be looked at but touched only by the priest.

There seems to be a closer relationship to the Lord and the people of the parish as a representative of the Lord during the Mass. This closeness becomes apparent when I hold the Body of Christ and distribute that same Body to the people.

There were two specific instances when this nearness to the Lord was especially felt. The initial occasion was when my children first received Communion from me, and I saw the tears in my wife's eyes when I lifted the host and said "The Body of Christ." The other situation was a Mass in which the congregation had the opportunity to receive under both species. As a minister

*of the cup for the first time, I felt, as I gazed into the cup,
his nearness in a way that is beyond description. It was
as if I could reach out and actually touch his face.*

*Every Sunday I pray that I may be worthy to
receive and distribute the host in a proper manner so
that when the day of judgment arrives, the Lord will
consider me worthy to enter his kingdom, and say to me:
"Enter my kingdom, my good and faithful servant."*

—*Don*

At the Last Supper, "Jesus took bread,
said the blessing, broke it, and giving it to his disciples said,
'Take and eat; this is my body.' Then he took a cup, gave
thanks, and gave it to them, saying, 'Drink from it, all of
you, for this is my blood....'"[1]

HISTORICAL BACKGROUND

These words are very familiar to us, as are the famous
paintings of that Holy Thursday event. It should be evident, then, that the meaning of Holy Communion is more
clearly signified when the faithful receive under both
kinds—when the members of a congregation not only eat
the Lord's Body, but actually drink his Blood under the
appearance of wine. It was because of this fuller sign value
that the Church from the outset until the beginning of the
second millennium in the West (and continuing on to the
present in the East) consistently and commonly distributed
Communion under both kinds to the laity. Throughout
those years and remaining today, this is the fullest expression and most perfect fulfillment of what our Lord said, did,
and directed: "Amen, amen, I say to you, unless you eat
the flesh of the Son of Man and drink his blood, you do not
have life within you."[2]

At the same time, the Church always gave Communion under one kind when circumstances so dictated, and it recognized this as a valid, complete, true sacrament. Thus, Christians received under the sign of bread alone when communicating at home or when the Eucharist was offered to the sick, to prisoners, or to monks living in isolation. Similarly, Communion under the appearance of wine alone for infants and the gravely ill formed a standard and accepted custom throughout this period.

Practical difficulties and poor attitudes linked to produce a change as the Church entered the second millennium. The change was not a denial, but in fact a greater affirmation of the truth that each kind, bread or wine, contained the whole Christ, present Body and Blood, soul and divinity, in all the fullness and power of his life, sufferings, and resurrection. But the faithful, for complicated historical reasons, approached the sacraments much less frequently and, unfortunately, failed to realize that the sacrifice and the sacrificial meal are one in the Mass. These doctrinal and devotional attitudes, combined with contagion in times of rampant diseases, the possibility of irreverence or spilling, the hesitation of some communicants to drink from the common cup, the large numbers at Easter and other special feasts, and the scarcity of wine in northern countries, led to a gradual abandonment of Communion under both kinds.

In the late eleventh century, the custom of distributing the Eucharist to the faithful under the form of bread alone began to grow. By the twelfth century some theologians even spoke of this as a canonical "custom" of the Church. The practice continued to spread until, in 1415, the Council of Constance decreed that Communion under the form of bread alone would be distributed to the faithful.[3]

A reaction soon set in and many Protestant reformers urged a return to the early Christian tradition. However, in doing so, some maintained that Communion under the sign of bread alone was invalid, a deprivation, an incomplete and erroneous fulfillment of the Lord's teaching in John's Gospel. The Roman Catholic Church reacted in face of those attacks and discouraged or forbade reintroduction of the practice under such doctrinal conditions.

VATICAN II–ROMAN MISSAL–NCCB

The Second Vatican Council decreed the restoration of this practice on occasions when it would be pastorally effective and spiritually beneficial. In doing so, however, a preparatory instruction was to make clear that, according to the Catholic faith, Christ is received whole and entire in a complete sacrament even when people communicate under one kind only. They are not, in such a circumstance, deprived of any grace necessary for salvation. Moreover, the catechesis should explain that the Church has the power to make laws about the administration of the sacraments and to change those regulations as long as they do not affect the very nature of the sacrament. Those alterations are dictated solely by what contemporary circumstances indicate is necessary for the reverence due to the sacrament and the spiritual good of the faithful. Finally, the Church explicitly encouraged the faithful to desire Communion under both kinds.

The revised Roman Missal specified fourteen cases when Communion might be distributed under both kinds. Later guidelines from the Congregation for Worship empowered the bishops of a country to extend this permission to other situations. The National Conference of Catholic Bishops in the United States, following those norms, in November 1970 added several instances to the list already determined by Rome. These included, among others, funerals, Masses for a special family observance, days of special religious or civil significance for the people of the United States, Holy Thursday, the Easter Vigil, and weekday Masses.[4]

Then in November 1978, the bishops of the United States voted to extend further the use of Communion under both kinds to the faithful at all Masses on Sundays and holy days of obligation. As in the other cases, this remains an option, with the decision when to offer Communion from the cup resting in the hands of the parish leadership. When a church decides to offer Communion under both species, the individual communicant should always be insured the freedom not to drink from the chalice.

The third typical edition of the *Roman Missal*, with its *General Instruction*, in 2002 gave Communion under both kinds even more generous application and endorsement with these words:

> Holy Communion has a fuller form as a sign when it is distributed under both kinds. For in this form the sign of the Eucharistic banquet is more clearly evident and clear expression is given to the divine will by which the new and eternal covenant is ratified in the Blood of the Lord, as also the relationship between the Eucharistic banquet and the eschatological banquet in the Father's kingdom.[5]

Practically speaking, current legislation now allows Communion from the cup on almost any occasion when it would be pastorally beneficial and can be administered with appropriate reverence.

SUPPORTIVE REASONS

No justification for Communion from the cup is truly needed other than the actual example of Jesus at the Last Supper and his command for us to do this in memory of him. Communicating under both kinds, we actually eat his Body *and* drink his Blood; we take and eat, take and drink. But there are additional reasons supportive of Communion from the chalice:

• The meal aspect of the Eucharist is more fully manifested.

• The connection between the eucharistic meal and the heavenly banquet in the Father's kingdom becomes easier to grasp. "I tell you, from now on, I shall not drink this fruit of the vine until the day when I drink it with you new in the kingdom of my Father."[6]

• It shows more clearly how the new and eternal covenant is ratified in the Blood of the Lord. We are thus forcefully reminded in the Mass itself of both Old and New Testament images that speak of an agreement sealed in blood between God and man:

> This is the cup of my blood, the blood of the new and everlasting covenant. It will be shed for you and for all so that sins may be forgiven.[7]

• Communion under both kinds recalls how the Mass has deep roots in the Passover meal, a ritual ceremony in which the drinking of wine took place at designated intervals and was accompanied by brief prayers or explanations. "The cup of blessing that we bless, is it not a participation in the blood of Christ?"[8]

- Receiving the Eucharist under the species of wine brings out the special, festive, joyful banquet notion of the Mass. We celebrate in the context of a sacred meal Jesus' and our resurrection from sin and death. Bread forms a staple item for meals in our culture, wine adds a dimension of specialness and festivity to the dinner. The psalmist proclaims: "You raise grass for the cattle, / and plants for our beasts of burden. / You bring bread from the earth, / and wine to gladden our hearts...."[9]

- Drinking from the chalice unites us to him who drank the cup of salvation and suffering.

When James and John, the sons of Zebedee, asked our Lord for preferred, privileged spots in his kingdom, Jesus told them, "You do not know what you are asking. Can you drink the cup that I shall drink or be baptized with the same baptism with which I am baptized?"[10]

Later on, in Gethsemane, Christ indicated by his words and example what he meant. Experiencing distress and with his heart "sorrowful even to death," says St. Matthew, Jesus said to Peter and the same James and John, "Remain here and keep watch with me." Then he "advanced a little and fell prostrate in prayer, saying, 'My father, if it is possible, let this cup pass from me; yet, not as I will, but as you will.'"

Some moments later, our Lord reiterated: "My Father, if it is not possible that this cup pass without my drinking it, your will be done!"[11]

- To drink from the cup reminds us we are by that action filled with the Holy Spirit.

St. Paul in his first letter to the Christians at Corinth warned the readers: "You cannot drink the cup of the Lord and also the cup of demons. You cannot partake of the table of the Lord and likewise the table of demons."[12]

Instead of being filled by evil spirits, we become in Communion filled with the Holy Spirit. Our eucharistic prayers explicitly state this: "Grant that we, who are nourished by his body and blood, may be filled with his Holy Spirit, and become one body, one spirit in Christ."[13] And "by your Holy Spirit, gather all who share this bread and wine into the one body of Christ."[14]

A patristic writer in the early Christian centuries spoke similarly: "Christ places two things before us: the bread and the chalice; and they are his body and blood...by which the grace of the Holy Spirit flows to us and nourishes us so as to make us immortal and incorruptible in hope."[15]

PRACTICAL IMPLEMENTATION

The *Roman Missal's General Instruction* offers several methods for receiving Communion under both kinds. However, the common acceptance of Communion in the hand, the lack of full sign value, and practical difficulties make procedures other than directly from the chalice not desirable as normal parish procedures. Our consideration here, therefore, will center on administration of the cup:

• The ministers of host and cup receive under both kinds from the presiding priest and/or other distributors, are given the designated vessels, and move to their posts. The chalice ministers should station themselves at some distance from their companion with the consecrated particles. This avoids confusion, permits lines to form without inconvenience, and allows the individual who chooses not to drink from the chalice easy freedom to return to his or her place in the congregation.

- The cup is offered to the communicant with the words "The blood of Christ," the person responding "Amen."

We might note, parenthetically, that the chalice is not to be left on the altar or passed from one communicant to another, nor should a communicant dip the host into the chalice.

- The cup should be totally handed over to the communicant, not merely tilted by the person drinking while being held by the minister. The latter procedure may be necessary for some exceptional cases (a small child, an incapacitated person, a parent with a baby in his or her arms), but the other process has been proven in practice to be superior.

- After the communicant has sipped some of the Precious Blood and returned the chalice, the minister wipes the rim with the purificator, turns the cup slightly, and offers it to the next person. We hardly need mention that these should be fresh, clean cloths for each or nearly every Mass, a requirement meaning that parishes must purchase an ample supply and arrange an efficient process for their laundering.

Some medical studies have indicated that this practice, plus the alcoholic content of the wine, minimizes the danger of communicating germs to others. Still, those with colds or other similar illnesses should naturally tend to refrain from drinking out of the cup. An occasional bulletin reminder about these studies and this common-sense caution could help allay some concerns in that regard.

• Children certainly may receive from the chalice, and some, experience shows, will make that choice. However, parents might give them the experience of drinking wine at home prior to Communion from the chalice and discuss how we use this in everyday life to mark a festive, joyous occasion or even as part of our daily food and drink.

Throughout this service to others, the distributor should reflect and radiate the qualities of prayerfulness, faith, and joy we discussed at length in the previous chapter.

Ministers of Mercy

As Catholics we believe that the smallest piece of the consecrated host is the Body and Blood of Jesus Christ: the same Jesus who was born in Bethlehem, was crucified, and who rose from the dead; the Jesus who is the Creator of the world. There are times when a sense of unworthiness overcomes me because of this realization. Yet, it is a tremendous privilege to be able to assist in the distribution of these hosts whether in church, or to those who are shut in at home or a special care facility. Often when bringing the Blessed Sacrament to those who are shut in at a nursing home, I sense the real presence of Jesus in a personal way. When the individual takes the host, their attention is on Jesus, for their God is with them now. One could say that a true friend came to visit.
—Michael

During several weekend Masses at Holy Cross Church in Vero Beach along Florida's east coast, a cluster of lay persons stand in the sanctuary after

Communion. A small plate with a white cloth and several sacred vessels rest upon the side of the altar. The vessels are circular containers, open and containing one or a few hosts; sometimes there is also a small bottle with wine. These have been present throughout the Liturgy of the Eucharist and thus are now the consecrated Body and Blood of Christ.

The presiding priest presents a pyx with hosts or a bottle with the Precious Blood to each of these extraordinary ministers of Communion and then recites this prayer blessing:

> Let us ask the Lord to look with kindness on the ministers of Holy Communion who have been entrusted to bring the life-giving Body and Blood of Christ to the sick and homebound members of the parish.
> May you go in peace.

These ministers of mercy leave the church and travel to homes, apartments, and institutions carefully carrying their sacred treasures to the sick and homebound. By following the official rite and the suggestions below, they in effect are bringing the Word and the Sacrament to those unable to participate at Sunday Mass in their local parishes. They, in fact, bestow many of God's choicest gifts upon those confined to their living quarters.

A CONTEMPORARY SHIFT

During the first decade after my ordination in 1956, a major priestly task for me and other clergy in pastoral ministry was to bring Holy Communion to the sick. We all had lists of these shut-ins and would faithfully visit them with the Eucharist each month. This list of names grew gradually until, after a dozen years at the Cathedral, it had reached a total of over seventy persons. I would arrange to cover perhaps a half-dozen over a morning or afternoon, allocating about fifteen minutes for each person.

This changed dramatically with the introduction in 1973 of extraordinary ministers of Holy Communion. Soon designated persons were visiting those same confined individuals with Holy Communion (although some people resisted this innovation at first and expressed a strong preference for the parish priest).

That introduction obviously eased the clergy's burden, but the extraordinary minister also could spend additional time with the homebound individual, visit more frequently, and even arrange to bring the Holy Eucharist to them on Sundays.

That rapid development made its way into the Church's ritual for the *Pastoral Care of the Sick.* Articles 72–73 of that document describe the ideal and practical ways this goal can be achieved:

> Priests with pastoral responsibilities should see to it that the sick or aged, even though not seriously ill or in danger of death, are given every opportunity to receive the Eucharist frequently, even daily, especially during the Easter season. They may receive communion at any hour. Those who care for the sick may receive communion with them, in accord with the usual norms. To provide frequent communion for the sick, it may be necessary to ensure that the community has a sufficient number of ministers of communion. The communion minister should wear attire appropriate to this ministry.
>
> The sick person and others may help to plan the celebration, for example, by choosing the prayers and readings. Those making these choices should keep in mind the condition of the sick person. The readings and the homily should help those present to reach a

deeper understanding of the mystery of human suffering in relation to the paschal mystery of Christ.

The faithful who are ill are deprived of their rightful and accustomed place in the eucharistic community. In bringing communion to them the minister of communion represents faith and charity on behalf of the whole community toward those who cannot be present at the Eucharist. For the sick the reception of communion is not only a privilege but also a sign of support and concern shown by the Christian community for its members who are ill.

The links between the community's eucharistic celebration, especially on the Lord's Day, and the communion of the sick are intimate and manifold. Besides remembering the sick in the general intercessions at Mass, those present should be reminded occasionally of the significance of communion in the lives of those who are ill: union with Christ in his struggle with evil, his prayer for the world, and his love for the Father, and union with the community from which they are separated.

The obligation to visit and comfort those who cannot take part in the eucharistic assembly may be clearly demonstrated by taking communion to them from the community's eucharistic celebration. This symbol of unity between the community and its sick members has the deepest significance on the Lord's Day, the special day of the eucharistic assembly.[1]

The rite is also very specific about ill persons unable to consume the consecrated hosts, but able to swallow the Precious Blood. It encourages and describes that process.

I remember well as a pastor doing just that for a woman whose throat cancer made consuming the host impossible, but who could swallow a small amount of the consecrated wine.

PASTORAL SUGGESTIONS

The procedure followed at Holy Cross in Vero Beach is really the ideal process for the reasons mentioned above in the excerpt from the *Pastoral Care* document.

Here are some additional suggestions:

Parish Connections. The ministers would do well to pick up a copy or copies of the weekly bulletin and bring these with them to the homebound. In addition, they might record the homily or at least make written or mental notes about its major points for use later at the home of those confined. Moreover, they may also recall any practical announcements made at the end of the Mass. This information would be communicated after the reading of Scripture and following the Communion Service.

Sacred Scripture. The ritual provides five brief excerpts from the Gospel and the first letter of John. As a praiseworthy alternative to these texts, a minister might bring his or her own Bible and read the Gospel designated for that particular Sunday.

General Intercessions. By paying close attention to the Prayer of the Faithful at Mass, ministers will have some ready-made intentions for the General Intercessions with the homebound.

Priest's Presence. Extraordinary ministers of Holy Communion are both desirable and necessary. But occasional or even regular visits by the parish priest are equally welcome and even essential. Those homebound persons always will gladly receive their shepherd and usually be most grateful for opportunities to receive the Sacraments of Penance and Anointing of the Sick.

Interested Listeners. Many of the homebound have few occasions to interact with others outside the immediate neighborhood. They thus normally will relish the occasion to visit at length with Communion ministers. Being interested listeners in such situations both fulfills Christ's command to love and greatly comforts those often-lonely persons confined at home.

A Healing Touch. Homebound individuals frequently feel isolated, cut off from the world that surrounds them. A light, gentle touch of hand, brow, or head from the eucharistic minister at some time during the visit helps bridge that gap and makes them feel connected with those outside the home.

The booklet *Communion of the Sick* (Catholic Book Publishing Company) contains the official ritual in both English and Spanish and the above suggestions. It also features three appendices: one describing the Prayer of the Faithful, another indicating the assigned liturgical Sundays through 2016, and a third giving the proper Gospel for each Sunday and several major feasts.[2] A pocket-sized New Testament combined with that ritual booklet should prove very beneficial in providing the proper Gospel for each visit.

Mercy, for most people, means forgiveness. However, a wider understanding of the term views mercy as embracing all of God's gifts for us. Consequently, extraordinary ministers of Communion to those who are ill or housebound can legitimately be called ministers of mercy.

8

Frequently Asked Questions I:
Theological Concerns

I read the invitation to an evening of reflection for those interested in becoming eucharistic ministers, and I was drawn to it. I was fairly new at Cathedral; I didn't know too many people by name, but I felt welcome and peaceful when I was there. The invitation came at a particularly challenging time in my life. I was a new principal, I was doing doctoral research, and most challenging of all, I was trying to raise a son in his tumultuous teens. Yet, every Sunday I was strengthened by early Mass in the company of my good sweet husband, a diverse and warm congregation, and a gentle, inspiring pastor.

The invitation tugged at me, but I was truly struggling to "keep it all together" and I was afraid that eucharistic ministers had it all together already. They were rock-solid people whose lives were in perfect or at least nearly perfect order. I, on the other hand, was still very much "under construction." But something, some longing made me go that night. Father gathered us in the

54

front pews of the church and centered us with a short meditation, and then he read from the Gospel about Jesus walking on the water during the storm and encouraging Peter to step out of the boat and come to him. I knew that it was the right place for me to be at that moment.

Being a eucharistic minister has meant so much to me. It has connected me to Our Lord in a very special way. It is a wordless connection, a holy intimacy that I can then share with the people of our parish. The moment when I offer them the cup of Our Lord's Precious Blood or place the Body of Christ in the palm of their hand is the most significant moment of their day, perhaps their week. And I have the honor of being part of that with them and with Our Lord. I try always to look in their eyes, to be aware of the magnitude of this sacrament for every person, to be reverent and welcoming at the same time. As I look into their faces, some old and tired, some young and anxious, I know that they, too, struggle with jobs and family and life. And as the Blessed Sacrament heals and strengthens me, it heals and strengthens them. I am honored and humbled to be a part of that.

—Donna

Over the past three decades serving either as pastor in three parishes or as a diocesan official, I have responded to many inquiries about extraordinary ministers of Holy Communion. Here are the most frequently asked questions with my brief response to each of them.

Question 1. What does "Let us proclaim the mystery of faith" said or sung at every Mass mean?

This statement invites us to express our belief in a central truth of the Catholic religion: Jesus came into the world, suffered, died, rose, and will come again in glory to judge the living and the dead at the end of time. We combine all those Christian events and term them the paschal or Passover mystery. They summarize the entire work of the Lord, his Good Friday and Easter passage from darkness and death to light and life, as well as what those saving actions make possible for us—our own Passover from the slavery of sinfulness to the freedom of grace.

Question 2. How does all of that relate to the Eucharist?

The Eucharist makes present in a mysterious manner the Last Supper, the sacrifice of Jesus' life poured out on Calvary, and the risen Lord's continued presence in our midst until this world ends. Thus, the mystery of faith mentioned in that invitation refers not only to Christ's actions in the past and future, but also to his presence here and now in the Mass.

Question 3. Are there other mysteries of our faith?

Many—for example, the Trinity, the blend of divine and human natures in Jesus, the Church, and the seven sacraments.

But the Church teaches that the eucharistic mystery is the true center of the whole Christian life; the other sacraments, even every activity of the Church, lead to the Eucharist and flow from it. The Eucharist can be compared to the sun drawing all other things to itself from which these receive their energy and power. The Eucharist contains not merely God's grace, but Christ himself.

Question 4. How can we better appreciate the eucharistic mystery?

We can never fully penetrate any of these divine mysteries, but by examining each one from different angles we are able to reach a deeper, richer understanding of them. Thus, to study separately the Eucharist from three points of view, as sacrifice, sacrament, and real presence, will help us grow in our comprehension of this, the greatest of mysteries in our Church, and also influence the way in which eucharistic distributors actually carry out their tasks.

Question 5. The Eucharist as sacrifice?

The Eucharist as sacrifice is the unbloody representation of Jesus' triumph, through his death and resurrection, over the powers of evil; it is the infinite worship of the Father in the Spirit through Christ the Savior; it is our most perfect way of praising God, humankind's most powerful prayer on earth.

This notion of the Eucharist as sacrifice has a practical application for eucharistic ministers: these persons need to bring an attitude of awe and worship to Mass, a spirit that will be evident not so much in the way they distribute the consecrated particles as the manner with which they conduct themselves during other parts of the liturgy.

Question 6. The Eucharist as sacrament?

The eucharistic mystery as sacrament is a nourishing spiritual food and drink, our divine daily bread.

For eucharistic ministers, that truth means, among other practical applications, this: Since Jesus gave us his Body and Blood under the signs of bread and wine in the context of a meal, the Lord must have expected that there would be accidents, that distributors or communicants, despite great caution, might occasionally drop a consecrated element or spill the blessed wine. Ministers thus should be careful but comfortable, reverent but relaxed.

Question 7. The Eucharist as real presence?

The Church teaches that the whole and entire Christ, divine and human, is substantially and permanently present in the consecrated bread and wine. It also praises a practice developed in the Middle Ages of adoring the Lord reserved in the tabernacle or exposed on the altar.

But the Church likewise cautions that the celebration of the Eucharist in the sacrifice of the Mass is truly the origin and the goal of the worship shown to the Eucharist outside Mass. Thus, adoring the Lord really present in the tabernacle should flow from and lead to the liturgy of the Mass.

Two recent changes in procedures instruct quietly, but symbolically and strongly, on finding the correct balance here; they also have some practical import for eucharistic ministers. The number of candles for Benediction or Exposition should be the same as for Mass (thus eliminating the 12–14 branch candelabra of former days), and a single genuflection only is made in the presence of the Blessed Sacrament whether reserved in the tabernacle or exposed for public adoration. The earlier double genuflection and multiple candles seemed to indicate erroneously that reservation, Exposition, or Benediction was superior in importance to Mass itself.

Question 8. What is the meaning of the term *concomitance*?

This heavy theological word expresses Catholic belief that the entire risen Jesus is present under the sign of either bread or wine and in each particle or portion of the consecrated element.

On the cross, Christ's Body and Blood were separated, his Blood poured out for our salvation. In the resurrection, however, they were mysteriously and gloriously reunited, never again to be divided. St. Paul tells us: "We know that Christ, raised from the dead, dies no more; death no longer has power over him."[1]

Consequently, whenever the priest pronounces the words, "This is my body," the Precious Blood of the Lord must necessarily be present. When he recites, "This is my blood," so, too, Jesus' risen body must automatically be there.

That truth of our faith carries with it certain very practical implications for both eucharistic ministers and for communicants.

Question 9. How does the notion of concomitance affect communicants?

It means that the entire Lord Jesus is received whether we communicate under the sign of bread alone, wine alone, or under both kinds. The Church encourages Communion from the chalice simply because it is a fuller, better sign of what the Lord did at the Last Supper and desires to do now. It does not, nevertheless, require that procedure for lay persons.

Thus, individuals who prefer not to receive under both kinds should simply pass by the offered cup and return to their places, reassured that they have not lost any grace by avoiding the chalice.

The notion of concomitance applies also to persons who because of some physical or emotional difficulty cannot receive under the sign of bread. They may communicate under the appearance of wine alone, also knowing that the total risen Lord has entered their hearts.

In my priesthood, as in the example noted earlier, I have served several infirm persons who no longer could swallow even a particle of the consecrated host, but were able to drink a portion of the Precious Blood.

Question 10. In the second situation, the sick receiving only under the sign of wine, from where does the priest secure the Precious Blood?

The priest consecrates the wine at Mass that day, usually in a small bottle, places the receptacle in the tabernacle until later, and then carries it in a special kit to the communicant. A special minister, of course, might fulfill this latter task.

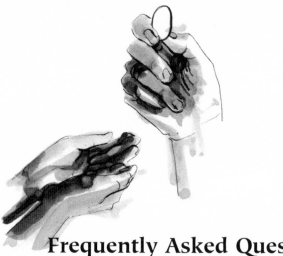

9

Frequently Asked Questions II: Pastoral Issues

Question 11. For how long is a minister commissioned?

The length of time depends on local arrangements. In some parishes for pastoral reasons the leaders place ministers on three-year terms that can be renewed. There are several advantages to such a procedure.

First, it enables individuals to terminate their ministries without uncomfortableness when personal reasons may so dictate. It could be somewhat awkward and could raise unanswerable questions to be forced to say to the pastor, "I wish to resign from my position as eucharistic minister."

Second, it opens the door for others to participate in this ministry.

Third, and perhaps most important, volunteers tend to be more faithful when duties accepted will be completed within a specific time frame.

Most bingo workers, for example, generally find themselves with an unspoken obligation or commitment that is expected, like the marriage promise, to be kept until death. In such never-ending arrangements, volunteers eventually grow weary. Rather than openly asking to resign, they often simply fail to show for their tasks with increasing frequency and eventually do not appear at all. That causes complex problems—operational ones for those in charge of the bingo games and emotional ones (guilt, uncomfortableness) for those who abandon their tasks.

A similar pattern for eucharistic ministers causes identical and perhaps more serious difficulties. Worship suffers because of the "no-shows." The enthusiastic spirit and reliable performance of the other ministers can deteriorate due to such spotty and wavering actions. Those who gradually, then totally, fall away from these responsibilities may later feel troubled spiritually because of this ministry's close relationship to their faith and their God.

Persons who study the habits of volunteers have concluded that three years appears to be the average length of time people serve effectively in a particular position. After that they usually require a shift to some other type of freely given service.

Question 12. Is lack of fidelity to their assignments on the part of eucharistic ministers a problem in parishes?

I have no statistics on that point, but given the weakness of human nature and the contemporary culture's change of attitude toward commitments, it would not be surprising.

In the beginning, of course, the newness and the awesomeness of this important office carries one along with fervor and dedication. But repetition can make even religious duties routine. Those activities we first approach with such reverence and care may, after repeated use, become ordinary and tiresome.

Likewise, when the duties of a eucharistic minister also begin to cause scheduling conflicts in family life or interfere with personal pleasure, fidelity becomes a challenge. Moreover, if several members of a family are involved in various weekend church activities at different Masses (eucharistic minister, lector, choir, nursery school, and so on), the struggle takes on further complications. It has been rumored that serving as the parish scheduling coordinator for eucharistic ministers constitutes one of the signs of sainthood, certainly of martyrdom.

Question 13. Am I commissioned only for my own parish or for any church?

The normal appointment is for service in one's own parish, not for the entire diocese or for the universal Church. On occasions in other places when the priest requests assistance from visitors who are already eucharistic ministers, he in effect is commissioning those individuals on the spot for that particular liturgy at that specific church.

Question 14. Why do some eucharistic ministers still feel unworthy and their fellow parishioners uncomfortable about lay persons or religious, that is, persons other than ordained priests and deacons, distributing Communion?

There is no simple and all-encompassing response to this question, but here are several factors that certainly contribute to the phenomenon: the long tradition of popular teaching on reverence due the Eucharist, which stressed that only the sacred hands of the priest may touch the host;

the continued negative attitude of some Catholics at Mass toward lay persons as extraordinary ministers; the general reaction of persons to any change that affects deeply personal patterns of believing, feeling, or acting.

Question 15. Since various secular changes in American life seem so frequent, desired, and expected, are Church changes that much of a problem?

For some and probably many, yes; at least in the beginning, changes within the Church have and can cause negative emotional reactions. Those hostile, angry, noncooperative responses are not, however, restricted to religious matters.

Alvin Toffler explains in his book *Future Shock* that when a new or novel idea, bit of information, sight, sound, or way of doing things enters our environment and challenges our preconceived worldview we can expect what he terms an "orientation response." That reaction will be psychosomatic, with the heart pumping faster, the stomach churning, the lungs breathing harder, and the blood rushing to our head; we sense an overall annoyed, confused, and uncomfortable feeling throughout our body.[1]

To verify this, the reader might reflect for a moment on some past experiences of his or her life connected with religion: a son moves in with his girlfriend; a daughter declares she likes women more than men; a teenager denies believing in God and protests going to church; friends, married many years, without warning break up; other couples make a marriage encounter and start holding hands at Communion; a neighbor becomes charismatic, acts differently, and tries to persuade all to make Jesus their personal friend.

When a neighbor down the street begins distributing Communion at Mass instead of only the priest offering the consecrated host, that shift in behavioral pattern, too, can trigger orientation responses.

An analysis of the same situation—the change process—but from a different perspective will lead to an identical conclusion. Recent research on the feelings of those who are dying or who care about the terminally ill reveals some commonly experienced feelings: denial, anger, bargaining, sadness, and acceptance. We now also recognize that parallel reactions may occur whenever a person experiences some deeply felt personal loss. Thus, a divorce, the sale of one's home, a job transfer, the breakup of a friendship, a pastor's departure, the death of a dream, a business failure, or the renovation of a parish church will very likely make individuals, at least for a time, sad and angry or lead them to deny the change or bargain with God for its postponement.

The introduction of persons other than priests as Communion distributors may, for some, be viewed as the parallel, painful death of an old, cherished tradition; they may see this as destruction of a religious principle learned early and held dear for a lifetime; finally, they may judge the innovation as another dangerous weakening of an unchangeable Church which, in their opinion, surely should remain unchanged in the turbulent, ever-changing world around them. Both the change and grieving processes take time for satisfactory resolution.

A survey in the 1970s indicated that 75 percent of American Catholics accepted the basic liturgical renovations of worship in the vernacular, Mass facing the people, guitar music, and so on. The same study revealed that only 45 percent approved of lay persons as eucharistic ministers. A survey today would probably discover that this 45 percent figure had risen to 75 percent or higher.

Question 16. Do those theories explain the rejection that eucharistic ministers sometimes receive at Sunday worship or outside church during the week?

They certainly would provide some explanation for such behavior. Eucharistic ministers have been told point-blank by neighbors or even friends, "I would never receive Communion from you"; they have observed parishioners walk completely out of their way and around the church to where a priest distributes the Eucharist; they have stood next to the celebrant and with him offered Communion, only to note two dozen waiting for priest and only two willing to approach the eucharistic minister; they have heard a father say, "I am glad you two (son and daughter-in-law) were appointed as Communion distributors, but I still don't like it."

Those kinds of negative actions can be painful and embarrassing for eucharistic ministers, but should not be interpreted as rejections of them as persons. They are, instead, merely ways through which some are dealing, in many instances unconsciously, with uncomfortable, angry, threatened, and confused feelings within themselves.

Great patience, accepting love, and inner strength and courage are called for here by both parish leaders and eucharistic ministers.

Question 17. Does the Church make any special spiritual or moral demands upon persons appointed as eucharistic ministers?

Yes. It insists that candidates should be noted for their Christian life and morals and that those commissioned must strive to be examples of Christian living in faith and conduct. Pope Paul VI in authorizing Communion distributors listed the qualities that, according to the ideal, should be present in the eucharistic minister. Finally, the priest who commissions eucharistic ministers addresses a spiritual challenge to them in the words of the ritual or with his own similar phrases.

Question 18. Aren't those unrealistic expectations an excessive burden for already reluctant and unsure candidates?

Perhaps, but that call to be examples of Christian living must be properly interpreted.

The Church well understands human weakness. It recognizes that we all sometimes fall short in our efforts to follow the Lord and often miss the mark morally and spiritually. Yet God works through wounded healers, earthen vessels, and fragile instruments.

The Church summons eucharistic ministers to be more, to become better persons, to strive for holiness, while at the same time it knows from two thousand years of history that all Christians, including or even especially leaders or ministers, never in this life perfectly attain those goals.

Question 19. What about blatantly bad, observable behavior on the part of eucharistic ministers?

That would be a different, unfortunate situation.

The Church urges eucharistic ministers to strive for sanctity, but it doesn't require that they be saints. Commissioned persons should not in any way judge that their appointment gives them special status or privileged rank above fellow parishioners. Nor does this position signify that their personal lives have been stamped with divine approval. The community of believers merely calls them to be servants, to serve their brothers and sisters in a humble way. Because of the dignity of this task—handling the holy Lord himself—they accept the ministry with a certain added responsibility to become holy themselves or at least as holy as possible.

Persons with noticeably and blatantly bad moral habits should not accept an appointment as eucharistic ministers, and those who slip into such faults after commissioning ought to take a leave from the ministry or resign entirely from it until this major weakness is corrected.

Otherwise they indeed may "cause scandal among the faithful" and their poor example may hurt rather than help eucharistic worship.

Question 20. Must eucharistic ministers wear any special vestments such as an alb?

The U.S. Bishops' Committee on the Liturgy has indicated that Communion distributors do not wear the liturgical vestments of an ordained deacon or priest, but instead should dress neatly in a way consonant with the importance of this function. Putting on one's best Sunday clothes for the occasion seems to represent a good guideline for the matter.

While the bishops left the question of the proper garb to local custom, and while some dioceses do provide identifying medals, pendant, jackets, or coats, the use of an alb or something similar raises certain difficulties. By clothing ministers in a way that makes them at least partially resemble the clergy, there is a danger that we may be minimizing the person's baptismal dignity and unconsciously or indirectly fostering a return to the notion that "only priests can touch the host." Eucharistic ministers are lay or religious men and women empowered by Christian initiation to distribute the Lord, not individuals elevated to the position of "little priests" and thereby worthy to fulfill this task.

Question 21. Do distributors wash their hands before Communion as the priest does at Mass?

No. We presume that their hands have been cleansed prior to Mass. When the priest washes his fingers or hands during the eucharistic liturgy, he performs a symbolic more than a practical gesture. "Lord, wash away my iniquity; cleanse me from my sin" are the words recited to accompany this action. The physical washing expresses a desire that God will likewise and more importantly grant spiritual cleansing of our sinful selves before we offer the sacrifice, receive Communion, or distribute the Eucharist. Ministers would do well to enter into the spirit of that ritual as the priest carries it out.

Question 22. Should ministers at every liturgy purify their fingers in the little cup or afterward in the sacristy?

These steps may be taken, but they need to be taken only when ministers detect noticeable particles remaining after the distribution of Communion.

Question 23. What must a minister do when someone drops a host or spills a bit of the Precious Blood?

There are so many variables in those situations that my only recommendation is: "Do the best you can." Despite care and reverence, such accidents will happen. If the consecrated host falls, the communicant or distributor generally will pick it up immediately and either consume, redistribute, or later dispose appropriately of the blessed particle. If the consecrated wine spills in any observable amount, the minister might place a purificator over the spot, obtain another linen, and later cleanse the location.

The *General Instruction of the Roman Missal* deals specially with this matter in article 280:

> If a host or any particle should fall, it is to be picked up reverently. If any of the Precious Blood is spilled, the area where the spill occurred should be washed with water, and this water should be poured into the sacrarium in the sacristy.

The *Norms for the Distribution and Reception of Holy Communion Under Both Kinds in the Dioceses of the United States of America* also discusses this concern in article 55:

> The reverence due to the Precious Blood of the Lord demands that it be fully consumed after Communion and never be poured into the ground or the sacrarium.

Question 24. What is the "sacrarium"?

The sacrarium is a specially constructed sink in the sacristy of the church that empties directly into the ground. Consecrated elements needing to be reverently discarded may be washed down the sacrarium.

Question 25. Should eucharistic ministers correct communicants or even refuse to give the consecrated elements to persons apparently lacking the proper attitude?

Never. That sounds harsh and absolute, but most priests for years have observed this sound pastoral principle: Do not embarrass anyone at Communion time. If there seems to be some question about the person's disposition or the manner of receiving, that should be discussed later, privately, by the priest with the individual.

When eucharistic ministers note on repeated occasions situations that appear to require some attention, they should simply speak to the pastor and let him take whatever steps he judges necessary.

For example, ministers may experience an increasing number of communicants inappropriately dipping the host into the chalice as described above, or observe youngsters who, reflecting a lack of training or perhaps even their non-Catholic status, irreverently receive Communion. Rather than mention this to them on the spot, the ministers would do well to make a mental note and relate their concerns afterward to the priest.

Question 26. What procedure do eucharistic ministers follow when they run out of consecrated hosts or the blessed wine has been depleted?

First of all, the ministers obviously would return to the altar or tabernacle and replenish the supply of consecrated hosts, if they are available. If not, they would, when sensing a potential shortage, begin early during the distribution of Communion to break the blessed bread into smaller particles. When the chalice of Precious Blood is empty, a minister immediately leaves the place of distribution and returns the cup to the proper location for cleansing the vessels.

Question 27. Is it proper for communicants to take the host in their hands, dip it into the chalice, and place the moistened particle in their mouths?

No. Communion through intinction by which the priest, deacon, or minister dips a host in the Precious Blood and offers this to the communicant with the accompanying words "The body and blood of Christ" does have approval from the universal Church. However, in the United States, because of the option for Communion in the hand, intinction has been discouraged. Moreover, the practice of the communicant dipping host described above has not received any official approbation, but rather explicit dis-couragement.

Question 28. Are there brief biblical passages to guide and support extraordinary ministers of the Eucharist?

Yes. These point to the need for a combination of humility and confidence. In Jesus' discourse about the vine and the branches, he said: "Whoever remains in me and I in him will bear much fruit, because without me you can do nothing."[2] "Without me you can do nothing" could be an inspirational motto for ministers of the Eucharist to repeat often in their hearts. It reminds us of why humility is an essential quality for all who serve at the altar.

Paul begged God three times for relief and release from the thorn in the flesh given to him, the angel of Satan beating him to keep Paul from being too elated over the revelations he had experienced. The Lord, however, did not accede to his request, but responded in this way: "My grace is sufficient for you, for power is made perfect in weakness."[3]

The Lord's words instilled confidence in Paul and should do the same for ministers of the Eucharist. Like "Without me you can do nothing," the phrase "My grace is sufficient for you," could be a companion inspirational motto to carry in their hearts and be repeated frequently.

10

Current Official Directives:
General Instruction of the Roman Missal

It's been so long, I'm trying to remember when I became a eucharistic minister!

In the beginning I was assigned to bring Communion to a household that included a young couple with three children, the grandparents, and a great grandfather. I brought Communion to the grandfather who had emphysema and the elderly great grandfather. I became "a part of the family." Later the young husband joined our first R.C.I.A. class at Cathedral and his wife and mother-in-law came to all the classes with him.

Later I was asked to bring Communion to a young girl who had Multiple Sclerosis and was confined to a wheelchair.

Both experiences are unforgettable.

Even after being a minister of Communion for over twenty years, I still feel the same awesome honor and privilege of bringing the Body and Blood of our Lord to others.

I truly believe *the Lord is present in the consecrated bread and wine, and place the host ever so gently and lovingly in the hand or on the tongue, and I pray: "Oh Lord, I am not worthy but thank you for allowing me to be an extension of your hands. By giving me this privilege, you are making me try all the harder to be more worthy."*

—Marge, who has served
as an extraordinary minister
of Holy Communion for
twenty-five years

I stood like a little child, in feeling and posture, on my first day administering the Eucharist. The feeling was overwhelming. I tried to be very cautious and alert as I felt I simply could not make a mistake. I also felt quite reverent as if God had put me here, in this cathedral, at this time, to do a very important job, to be his servant and to serve others in this precious and most sacred way. What a privilege to be a modern-day lay minister and in so doing strengthen my understanding and appreciation of our faith. I am most grateful but also very undeserving. May God grant me the grace to continue in my journey back to the Lord.

—Frank, who began this
ministry four months ago

In recent years the Church, on the universal and the national level, has issued several liturgical documents that impact the way in which ministers of Holy Communion distribute the Body and Blood of Christ.

These include, among others, the following documents arranged chronologically:

1980   *Norms for the Worship of the Eucharistic Mystery*

1983   *Holy Communion Outside Mass*

1998   *On Keeping the Lord's Day Holy*

2002   *Norms for the Distribution and Reception of Holy Communion Under Both Kinds in the Dioceses of the United States of America*

2003   *Ecclesia de Eucharistia (On the Eucharist)*, Encyclical Letter of Pope John Paul II

2003   *Spiritus et Sponsa,* "The Spirit and the Bride," Apostolic Letter of Pope John Paul II

2003   *General Instruction of the Roman Missal* (Third Typical Edition)

2003   *Introduction to the Order of Mass: A Pastoral Resource of the Bishops' Committee on the Liturgy*

2003   *Redemptionis Sacramentum (Sacrament of Redemption)*, an Instruction by the Congregation for Divine Worship and the Discipline of the Sacraments

Two of these most current texts, *General Instruction of the Roman Missal* and *Introduction to the Order of Mass,* have been published in attractive paperback by the United States Conference of Catholic Bishops Publishing Service in Washington, DC. Ministers of Holy Communion could, of course, benefit from reading both documents in their entirety and reflecting upon them. However, to assist those for whom such a study is not feasible, we have here excerpted from both documents those articles or sections that have particular relevance today for extraordinary ministers of Holy Communion. Some items will merely be a review of what ministers have been doing, others represent a change in procedure, and still others should serve to renew the spirit with which ministers perform this sacred ministry.

Monsignor James Maroney, the Executive Director of the USCCB Secretariat for the Liturgy, notes in his introductory comments that the *Introduction to the Order of Mass* is a pastoral resource, not a legislative or judicial document. The *Roman Missal,* including the rubrics found in the *Order of Mass* and the *General Instruction,* is "the authentic source for what the Church requires in the celebration of the Sacred Liturgy."[1] However, the *Introduction to the Order of Mass,* approved by the American bishops, still will be a very helpful tool in training various liturgical ministers. The Prefect of the Roman Congregation for Divine Worship declares that it will be "a useful pastoral instrument for liturgical formation of the People of God."[2]

We will first cite a half-dozen pertinent articles from the *General Instruction* and then in the next chapter turn to the *Introduction* for three dozen items of special interest. In most instances we will cite the text exactly and in a few others for the sake of brevity paraphrase the content (without quotation marks).

GENERAL INSTRUCTION OF THE ROMAN MISSAL (THIRD TYPICAL EDITION)

In 1570 the Church issued a *Roman Missal* that served as the basis for Masses in the Western Rite of the Catholic Church for four hundred years. In 1970, the Church issued the First Edition of a revised *Roman Missal* with a lengthy *General Instruction* containing detailed guidelines for the celebration of Mass. This implemented the directives of the Second ·Vatican Council given in the *Constitution on the Sacred Liturgy* (1963). In 2002, the Church issued a Third Edition of this restored *Roman Missal.*

The changes in that Third Edition are few and relatively minor, but still of significance, and they do impact the way in which we celebrate the Holy Eucharist.

It should be noted at the outset that the *General Instruction* designates lay persons who are deputed to distribute Holy Communion as *extraordinary ministers.* This designation differentiates them from the ordinary ministers of Holy Communion who are bishops, priests, and deacons (no. 100).

The *General Instruction* contains two lengthy articles about *silence* within the liturgy—sections 45 and 56. In no. 56, it speaks of the need for meditative silence during the Liturgy of the Word; in no. 45, it directs that sacred silence be observed at designated times during Mass, then lists those occasions and the purpose of the silence at such moments.

In the second paragraph of no. 45, the *General Instruction* offers this practical suggestion:

> Sacred silence also, as part of the celebration, is to be observed at the designated times. Its purpose, however, depends on the time it occurs in each part of the celebration. Thus within the Act of Penitence and again after the invitation to pray, all recollect themselves; but at the conclusion of a reading or the homily, all meditate briefly on what they have heard; then after Communion, they praise and pray to God in their hearts.

150. A little before the consecration, when appropriate, a server rings a bell as a signal to the faithful. According to local custom, the server also rings the bell as the priest shows the host and then the chalice.

If incense is used, a server incenses the host and the chalice when each is shown to the people after the consecration.

280. If a host or any particle should fall, it is to be picked up reverently. If any of the Precious Blood is spilled, the area where the spill occurred should be washed with water, and this water should then be poured into the sacrarium in the sacristy.

281. Holy Communion has a fuller form as a sign when it is distributed under both kinds. For in this form the sign of the Eucharistic banquet is more clearly evident and clear expression is given to the divine will by which the new and eternal Covenant is ratified in the Blood of the Lord, as also the relationship between the Eucharistic banquet and the eschatological banquet in the Father's Kingdom.

282. Sacred pastors should take care to ensure that the faithful who participate in the rite or are present at it are as fully aware as possible of the Catholic teaching on the form of Holy Communion as set forth by the Ecumenical Council of Trent. Above all, they should instruct the Christian faithful that the Catholic faith teaches that Christ, whole and entire, and the true Sacrament, is received even under only one species, and consequently that as far as the effects are concerned, those who receive under only one species are not deprived of any of the grace that is necessary for salvation.

Paragraph 283 outlines occasions at which *Communion under both kinds* is permitted, but then includes in its final paragraph mention of legislation *for this nation* (which is more expansive in its permission) contained in *Norms for the Distribution and Reception of Holy Communion Under Both Kinds in the Dioceses of the United States of America.*

11

A Pastoral Resource:
Introduction to the Order of Mass

In 1997 the United States Conference of Bishops approved the *Introduction to the Order of Mass*. It was revised in 2000 by the Vatican Congregation for Divine Worship and the Discipline of the Sacraments in the light of changes introduced by the Third Edition of the *Roman Missal*. The American bishops then approved the emended version and published it in 2003 with a subtitle: *A Pastoral Resource of the Bishops' Committee on the Liturgy.*

The book contains a wealth of practical suggestions and inspirational concepts. Both are needed and welcomed. As its introduction states, "Good liturgy is the product not so much of a well-known rubric as much as a well-trained heart."[1]

In this chapter, we quote here at length articles or sections that are particularly relevant for extraordinary ministers of Holy Communion. Therefore the rest of this chapter comes directly from the *Introduction to the Order of Mass.*

9. Opportunities should be made available periodically for liturgical ministers to pray together and to receive continuing formation for their tasks. These occasions may provide for their ongoing training and for the improvement of their abilities to facilitate the liturgical celebration.

10. Liturgical ministers are to give care to the verbal and physical elements of the liturgy. Thus by reverent posture, gesture, and movement, they reinforce the words of the liturgy and help facilitate the faithful's response. When not performing particular duties, they join the rest of the congregation by listening, responding, and singing, thereby contributing to the whole body's worship.

13. In the Liturgy of the Eucharist, the deacon helps to distribute Holy Communion to the people, especially as minister of the chalice. In this connection, he also prepares the table and gifts, elevates the chalice at the doxology, and may assist with the breaking of the bread....

17. The liturgical assembly is not a random group of individuals but is, rather, the gathering of God's people to exercise its royal priesthood in the sacrifice of praise. Its structure and ordering are a reflection of the Church herself, governed and served by the Bishop, priests and deacons. The celebration is organized to encourage and foster an awareness of the liturgical assembly's common dependence on God and each other as well as its common dignity and purpose.

Singing and uniformity in posture and gesture expresses and deepens that communal dimension of worship. Moreover, accommodation for people with special needs and the special inclusion of children in the celebrations further fosters this communal element of the liturgy.

19. The Body and Blood of Christ should be received as spiritual food by all those properly disposed since the Eucharistic celebration is the Paschal banquet. When there are large numbers, the priest may need assistance in distributing Holy Communion so that the rite is not unduly long.

20. Bishops, priests, and deacons are the ordinary ministers of Holy Communion. Instituted acolytes, when available, may assist as extraordinary ministers. Occasionally, however, this assistance will be given by other extraordinary ministers of Holy Communion, either formally commissioned for a given period or, in case of necessity, deputed as needed by the priest celebrant.

21. These ministers serve Christ present in the gathered assembly by ministering his Body and Blood to their brothers and sisters. They also serve the unity of the worshiping community by taking Holy Communion to those members who are prevented by sickness, old age, or other cause from taking part in the congregation. In accord with an ancient tradition, it is appropriate for Holy Communion to be taken directly from the Sunday Mass to the sick and to those unable to leave their homes.

Those carrying out the various liturgical roles need not be accommodated in the sanctuary for the whole celebration. The extraordinary ministers of Holy Communion come forward from their place among the people after the reception of Holy Communion by the priest celebrant.

After the Communion of the priest, the extraordinary ministers receive Communion from him. Then they receive the Sacred Vessels with the Body or Blood of the Lord for distribution to the faithful. Extraordinary ministers of Holy Communion never receive Holy Communion in the manner of concelebrants.

The deacon or concelebrating priests assist in the preparation of the Eucharistic bread and chalices for Holy Communion. If it is necessary to use the hosts consecrated from a previous Mass, a priest or deacon should bring the reserved sacrament to the altar from the tabernacle, reverently but without ceremony.

When the distribution of Holy Communion is complete, the deacon and the concelebrating priests—or, in their absence, the acolytes or other extraordinary ministers of Holy Communion—should return the Sacred Vessels to the altar, where the priests or deacons gather into one or more ciboria any remaining Sacred Hosts and then place them in the tabernacle. The Sacred Vessels are then brought to the altar or a side table. When more of the Precious Blood remains than was necessary for Communion, and if it is not consumed by the Bishop or priest celebrant, the deacon immediately and reverently consumes at the altar all of the Blood of Christ that remains; he may be assisted, if needed, by other deacons and priests. When extraordinary ministers of Holy Communion are present, they may consume what remains of the Precious Blood from their chalice of distribution. The Sacred Vessels should be purified by a priest, deacon, or instituted acolyte immediately or be left to be purified as soon as Mass has been completed. The faculty may be given by the diocesan Bishop to the priest celebrant to be assisted, when necessary, even by extraordinary ministers of Holy Communion in the cleansing of the vessels after the distribution of Communion.

When Holy Communion is being taken from Mass to the sick or those unable to leave their homes, the priest gives the pyx containing the Holy Eucharist to the deacons, acolytes, or extraordinary ministers of Holy Communion immediately after Communion has been distributed. Alternatively they may depart immediately after receiving Communion themselves, or even as part of the concluding procession of ministers.

24. "In the Liturgy the sanctification of women and men is given expression in symbols perceptible by the senses and is carried out in ways appropriate to each of them." Taking bread and wine, pronouncing over these elements the words of Christ, and then breaking the bread and giving these Eucharistic elements to the faithful all constitute the principal symbolism of the Sacred Liturgy. The importance of this symbolism is further emphasized and conveyed by the entire ritual complex of words and actions set forth in the liturgical books authoritatively promulgated by the Church. Consequently, it is important that these actions be carried out in a correct and dignified manner so that they will truly be seen as actions of the Church herself in conformity with the will of Christ. Words clearly proclaimed, actions deliberately and gracefully performed, and elements and objects authentically made and reverently handled contribute to the integrity of the liturgy and allow its symbolism to work to greater effect.

31. One kneels as a human gesture of submission. In Christian tradition, kneeling is an acknowledgment of one's creatureliness before God. It can signify penitence for sin, humility, reverence, and adoration.

● The United States Conference of Catholic Bishops (USCCB) may adapt the actions and postures described in the *Order of Mass,* in accord with local sensibilities and the meaning and character of the rite. The *recognitio* of the Holy See is required for such adaptations to take effect.

• Accordingly, the USCCB has decided that, in general, the directives of the *Roman Missal* should be left unchanged but that paragraph no. 43 of the *General Instruction of the Roman Missal* should be adapted so that the people sit for the readings before the Gospel reading, for the Responsorial Psalm, and for the homily and the Preparation of the Gifts; and they may sit or kneel during the period of religious silence after Communion, if doing so seems helpful. They should kneel beginning after the singing or recitation of the *Sanctus* (or "Holy, Holy") until after the Amen of the Eucharistic Prayer, except when prevented on occasion because of health, lack of space, the large number of people, or some other good reason. Those who do not kneel ought to make a profound bow when the priest genuflects after the consecration. The faithful kneel after the *Agnus Dei* (or "Lamb of God") unless the diocesan Bishop determines otherwise.

47. Silence is, as in all communication, a most important element in the communication between God and the community of faith. Its purpose is to allow the voice of the Holy Spirit to be heard in the hearts of the People of God and to enable them to unite personal prayer more closely with the word of God and the public voice of the Church. During liturgical silence, all respond in their own way: recollecting themselves, pondering what has been heard, petitioning and praising God in their inmost spirit.

48. Liturgical silence is not merely an absence of words, a pause, or an interlude. Rather, it is a stillness,

a quieting of spirits, a taking of time and leisure to hear, assimilate, and respond. Any haste that hinders reflectiveness should be avoided. The dialogue between God and the community of faith taking place through the Holy Spirit requires intervals of silence, suited to the congregation, so that all can take to heart the word of God and respond to it in prayer.

50. The very nature of sacramental symbolism demands that the elements for the Eucharist be recognizable, in themselves and without explanation, as food and drink, while the authenticity of sacramental celebration demands that the elements for the Eucharist follow the unvarying tradition of the Latin Church.

● Bread should be recently made from wheat flour, should be unleavened and free from any foreign substance, and should "have the appearance of food." In other words, it should be identifiable as bread by means of its consistency—that is, its color, taste, texture, and smell—while its form should remain the traditional one.

● Wine should be natural and pure, the fermented juice of the grape, and similarly free from any foreign substance.

51. Sacred Vessels for the Eucharistic elements should be made of noble metals, gilded on the inside unless they are made of gold or a more noble metal, in a form consistent with local usage and with their function in the liturgy. They should be clearly distinguishable from objects in everyday use and be reserved exclusively for the liturgy. In the dioceses of the United States of America, Sacred Vessels may also be made from other solid materials that, according to the common estimation in each region, are precious—for example, ebony or other hard woods—provided that

such materials are suitable for sacred use and do not break easily or deteriorate. This applies to all vessels that hold the hosts: such as the paten, the ciborium, the pyx, the monstrance, and so on.

● The fundamental Eucharistic symbolism of many sharing in the one bread and one cup is more clearly expressed when all the bread is contained in a single vessel and all the wine in one vessel. Until the chalice is brought to the altar for the Preparation of the Gifts, it is fittingly covered with a veil, which may be white or else the color of the day....

● Sacred Vessels for the distribution of the Body of Christ preferably have the form of patens and ciboria rather than of chalices. Chalices for the Blood of Christ need to be large enough to be shared, easily handled between minister and communicant, and easily tilted by the communicant for drinking.

● A suitable pitcher and basin may be used for the washing of the priest's hands. The water intended to be mixed with the wine should be contained in a smaller, separate vessel appropriate for that purpose. Generous quantities of water and a towel will be necessary if the priest is to do more than wet the tips of his fingers.

52. Out of respect for Christ's memorial banquet, the altar is adorned with a covering both during and after Mass. This cover may be a cloth that covers only the top of the altar, or it may envelop the altar more fully. While the principal altar cloth is to be white, other cloths of colors that possess special religious, honorific, or festive significance according to long-standing local usage may be employed, or frontals may also be used. However, the uppermost cloth covering the mensa (i.e., the altar cloth itself) is always white in color. The shape, size, and decoration of the altar cloth should be in keeping with the design of the altar.

The fabric for altar cloths should be of good quality, design, and texture. At the Preparation of the Gifts, one or more corporals—large enough to accommodate the Sacred Vessels brought to the altar at the Preparation of the Gifts—are spread on top of the altar.

● Candles are used to express both reverence and festivity. They should be authentic and be made of a substance that gives a living flame and is seen to be consumed in giving its light. The candles may be placed on the altar or, more appropriately, near or around it, so as not to distract from the Sacred Vessels or impede the participants' view of the liturgical action.

● The top of the altar itself holds only what is necessary for the celebration—for example, the Sacred Vessels and *Roman Missal*—and those things remain on the altar only while needed. Decorative items like flowers may be placed near or around the altar, but not on it.

57. In the dioceses of the United States of America, acolytes, altar servers, lectors, and other lay ministers may wear the alb or other appropriate and dignified clothing.

61. The liturgical celebrations of culturally and ethnically mixed groups require special attention. Weekday Masses; celebrations with smaller groups; celebrations outside churches or chapels; Masses with children, young people, the sick, or persons with disabilities; and ritual Masses (for example, funeral or wedding Masses) at which a significant number of the congregation may be non-Catholics or otherwise not able in law to receive Holy Communion will necessarily impose different demands appropriate to the needs of the occasion.

In order to make clear the law of the Church on this matter, the Bishops of the United States of America issued in 1997 the following guidelines for receiving Holy Communion:

For Catholics—As Catholics, we fully participate in the celebration of the Eucharist when we receive Holy Communion. We are encouraged to receive Communion devoutly and frequently. In order to be properly disposed to receive Communion, participants should not be conscious of grave sin and normally should have fasted for one hour. A person who is conscious of grave sin is not to receive the Body and Blood of the Lord without prior sacramental confession except for a grave reason when there is no opportunity for confession. In this case, the person is to be mindful of the obligation to make an act of perfect contrition, including the intention of confessing as soon as possible (see CIC, c. 916). A frequent reception of the sacrament of Penance is encouraged for all.

For our fellow Christians—We welcome our fellow Christians to this celebration of the Eucharist as our brothers and sisters. We pray that our common Baptism and the action of the Holy Spirit in this Eucharist will draw us closer to one another and begin to dispel the sad divisions which separate us. We pray that these will lessen and finally disappear, in keeping with Christ's prayer for us "that they may all be one" (John 17:21).

Because Catholics believe that the celebration of the Eucharist is a sign of the reality of oneness of faith, life, and worship, members of these churches with whom we are not yet fully united are ordinarily not admitted to Holy Communion. Eucharistic sharing in exceptional circumstances by other Christians requires permission according to the directives of the diocesan Bishop and the provisions of canon law (c. 844 § 4). Members of the Orthodox Churches, the Assyrian Church of the East, and the Polish National Catholic Church are urged to respect the discipline of their own Churches. According to Roman Catholic discipline, the Code of Canon Law does not object to the reception of Communion by Christians of these Churches (c. 844 § 3).

For those not receiving Holy Communion— All those who are not receiving Holy Communion are encouraged to express in their hearts prayerful desire for unity with the Lord Jesus and with one another.

For non-Christians—We would welcome to this celebration those who do not share our faith in Jesus Christ. While we cannot admit them to Holy Communion, we ask them to offer their prayers for the peace and unity of the human family.

101. The Church encourages the faithful to bring forward the elements through which Christ's offering will be made present, together with money and other gifts for the sustenance of Christ's body, especially the poor and the needy.

103. First, the altar, the Lord's table, is prepared as the center of the Eucharistic liturgy.
   • Everything indicates that a new and important stage of the liturgy is about to begin. One or more corporals of sufficient size to accommodate all the Sacred Vessels that may be brought to the altar now are laid out.
   • The corporal, purificators, and *Roman Missal* are needed for the Eucharistic offering. They are not themselves offerings or gifts and are not brought up in the procession of gifts. Instead, they should be

brought reverently but without ceremony from a side table, along with the chalice if it will be prepared at the altar.

• Since these are preparatory tasks, they are carried out by a deacon, acolyte, or other minister or by other members of the congregation.

105. The elements of bread and wine are carried in the *procession* in vessels that can be easily seen. If possible, the bread and wine should each be contained in a single vessel, so that priest and people may be seen to be sharing the same food and drink in the sacrament of unity.

• The gifts of bread, wine, and money are carried forward by members of the congregation. The congregation's identification with the gifts is best expressed if the procession passes right through their midst. The gifts are accepted by the priest, who may be assisted by the deacon and other ministers. The collection of money and other gifts is deposited near the altar or in another suitable place. The priest places only the Sacred Vessels containing the bread and wine on the altar.

126. The community of the baptized is constituted as the family of God by the Spirit of adoption. In the fullness of this Spirit, who has once again been invoked upon them, they call upon him as Father. Because of its themes of daily bread and mutual forgiveness, the Lord's Prayer has been used in all liturgical traditions as a most appropriate preparation for Holy Communion, "so that what is holy may, in fact, be given to those who are holy." The final petition is expanded into a prayer that concludes with the congregational doxology or acclamation "For the kingdom," which was appended to the Lord's Prayer in some of the earliest liturgical texts and in texts of the New Testament.

129. The priest may give the sign of peace to the ministers, but he always remains within the sanctuary, so as not to disturb the celebration. In the dioceses of the United States of America, with good reason on special occasions (for example, at a funeral or wedding, or when civic leaders are present), the priest may offer the sign of peace to a few faithful near the sanctuary. All exchange the sign of peace with those nearest to them. The greeting "May the peace of the Lord be always with you" may be used, with the response "Amen."

130. *(Breaking of the Bread)* This characteristic action of Christ at the feeding of the multitude, at the Last Supper, and at his meals with the disciples after his resurrection in the days of the Apostles gave its name to the entire celebration of the Eucharist. The natural, the practical, the symbolic, and the spiritual are all inextricably linked in this most powerful symbol. Just as many grains of wheat are ground, kneaded, and baked together to become one loaf, which is then broken and shared out among many to bring them into one table-fellowship, so those gathered are made one body in the one bread of life that is Christ (see 1 Cor 10:17).

131. In order for the meaning of this symbolism to be perceived, both the bread and the breaking must be truly authentic and recognizable. The Eucharistic bread is to "have the appearance of food" and is to be made so that it can be broken and distributed to at least some of the members of the congregation.

● The faithful are *not ordinarily* to be given Holy Communion *from the tabernacle* with hosts consecrated at a previous Mass. When, for genuine pastoral reasons—for example, the late arrival of unexpected numbers—the hosts consecrated at the Mass must be supplemented with reserved consecrated hosts from the tabernacle, these hosts may be brought reverently but without ceremony from the tabernacle to the altar at the breaking of the bread.

• The bread is broken with dignity and delibera-tion, normally by the priest celebrant, who may be assisted by the deacon or a concelebrant. It begins after the exchange of peace is finished and when the attention of the faithful is again focused on the action taking place at the holy table.

• The regular use of larger breads will foster an awareness of the fundamental symbolism in which all, priest and people, share in the same host. At every Mass, at least one large host is broken into several portions. One of these portions is consumed by the priest, while the rest are distributed to at least a few others.

• During the breaking of the bread, the *Agnus Dei* ("Lamb of God") is sung or said. All call on Christ Jesus as the Lamb of God (see John 1:29, 36) who has conquered sin and death (see 1 Pet 1:18 and Rev 5:6, 13:8). The *Agnus Dei* is a litany intended to accom-pany the action of breaking and may therefore be pro-longed by repetition until such time as the action is completed.

• If extraordinary ministers assist in the distribu-tion of Holy Communion, they come to the altar after the communion of the priest.

133. The consecrated elements are raised up and shown to the people using the words that express the confidence of the baptized and to which they respond with the humility of the centurion (see Matt 8:9). The priest celebrant takes the host and elevates it above the paten or chalice in a gesture that is demonstrative and dignified.

134. Faithful to the Lord's command to his disciples to "take and eat" and "take and drink," the congregation completes the Eucharistic action by eating and drinking together the Body and Blood of Christ consecrated during the celebration. For this reason, the faithful should not ordinarily be given Holy Communion from the tabernacle. Also for this reason, for the faithful to share the chalice is most desirable, insofar as this is provided for by the norms of the Holy See, the diocesan Bishop, and the USCCB. Drinking at the Eucharist is a sharing in the sign of the new covenant (see Luke 22:20), a foretaste of the heavenly banquet (see Matt 26:29), a sign of participation in the suffering Christ (see Mark 10:38–39).

135. Although a communion procession is not obligatory and is not always possible, it should be the normal arrangement for both practical and symbolic reasons. It expresses the humble patience of the poor moving forward to be fed, the alert expectancy of God's people sharing the paschal meal in readiness for their journey, the joyful confidence of God's people on the march toward the promised land. The dioceses of the United States of America are given four options for the communion song.

136. A sufficient number of ministers should assist in the distribution of Holy Communion.
 • In all that pertains to Communion under both kinds, *Norms for the Distribution and Reception of Holy Communion Under Both Kinds in the Dioceses of the United States of America* is to be followed. When Holy Communion is administered under both kinds, the deacon who ministers the chalice is to receive Holy Communion from the priest under both kinds and then administer the chalice to the faithful; after the distribution of Holy Communion, he then reverently

consumes any of the Precious Blood left in the chalice, being assisted, if necessary, by other deacons and priests. If many priests are concelebrating, the Communion of the congregation need not be delayed but may begin after the presiding celebrant has communicated. There is no need for all the concelebrating priests to finish receiving Holy Communion before distribution to the congregation can commence, as long as the concelebrants are able to continue receiving Communion while it is also being distributed to the faithful.

• Extraordinary ministers of Holy Communion are *not* permitted to receive Holy Communion after the manner of the concelebrants (i.e., to self-communicate); instead they are to be given Holy Communion by one of the ordinary ministers of the sacrament.

• In the United States of America, Holy Communion may be received in the hand as well as on the tongue; the choice is the prerogative of the communicant. The faithful are not permitted to take up the consecrated bread or the sacred chalice themselves and still less to hand them to one another.

• Children, like adults, have the option to receive Holy Communion in the hand or on the tongue. No limitations because of age have been established. Careful preparation for first reception of the Eucharist will provide the necessary instruction.

• When receiving the Eucharist in the hand, the communicant approaches the minister with one hand resting on the palm of the other. After responding "Amen" the communicant steps to the side and reverently places the Eucharist in his or her mouth.

• When Holy Communion is distributed under both kinds by intinction, the Eucharist is not placed in the hands of the communicants, nor may the communicants receive the Eucharist and then dip it into the chalice themselves. In distributing Holy Communion by intinction, the minister says, "The body and blood of Christ," and the communicant responds, "Amen." Intinction should not be introduced as a means of circumventing the practice of taking Communion in the hand.

● When the USCCB and the diocesan Bishop have determined, in conformity with the norms set forth by the Holy See, that Communion under both kinds may be given, the pastor or priest celebrant should see to its full and proper implementation. Even when Communion is given under both kinds, however, the communicant may choose not to drink from the chalice.

● The norm for the posture of reception of Holy Communion in the dioceses of the United States is standing. However, communicants who kneel should not be denied Holy Communion because they kneel. Rather, such instances should be addressed pastorally, by providing the faithful with proper catechesis on the reasons for this norm.

● When receiving Holy Communion standing, the communicant bows his or her head before the sacrament as a gesture of reverence and receives the Body of the Lord from the minister. When Holy Communion is received under both kinds, the sign of reverence is also made before receiving the Precious Blood.

137. The communion song begins while the priest is receiving Holy Communion.

● So as not to encumber the congregation with books or scripts during the procession, the singing may be led by cantor or choir and include a repeated response from the congregation.

● Although several communion songs may be sung in succession, depending on the length of Communion, it may be preferable to interrupt congregational singing with periods of silence, instrumental music (in seasons when it is not excluded), or choral music, resuming the singing after an interlude.

• Some traditional Eucharistic hymns that were composed for Benediction of the Most Blessed Sacrament—and therefore concentrate on adoration rather than on the action of Communion—may not be appropriate as communion songs.

138. When the distribution of Holy Communion is completed, the altar is cleared and the Sacred Vessels are purified.

• Although performed with reverence, the purification should be done briefly and inconspicuously; especially if several Sacred Vessels must be purified, they may be covered, placed on a corporal at a side table, and purified as soon as possible after Mass.

• This purification—by a priest, deacon, or instituted acolyte—is carried out, if possible, at the side table. However, if necessary it may be done at the altar—and, if so, at the side of the altar rather than at the center.

• Pouring the Precious Blood into the ground or into the sacrarium is strictly prohibited.

139. After the distribution of Holy Communion, all may observe a period of silence. The absence of all words, actions, music, or movement offers an opportunity for interior prayer and contemplation on the Eucharistic mystery. Such silence is important to the rhythm of the whole celebration and is welcome in a busy and restless world.

• Silence and true stillness can be achieved if all take part—congregation and liturgical ministers alike.

• This period of deep and tranquil communion is not to be interrupted by the taking of a second collection or by parish announcements, which (if needed) come correctly in the concluding rite. Nor should this silence be broken or overlaid by the public reading or recitation of devotional material.

● As an alternative or addition to silent contemplation, a psalm or other song of praise may be sung.

Appendix

Shortly after I had completed this book, the Roman Congregation for Divine Worship and the Discipline of the Sacraments, following an extended consultation with the Congregation for the Doctrine of the Faith, issued on March 25, 2004, the Instruction *Redemptionis Sacramentum (Sacrament of Redemption)*.

This 58-page, 186-article document carries a subtitle, "On certain matters to be observed or to be avoided regarding the Most Holy Eucharist." The entire text, therefore, naturally impacts extraordinary ministers of Holy Communion. However, certain articles and an entire section directly pertain to them. For those reasons we have added this Appendix summarizing that Instruction.

BACKGROUND

On April 17, 2003, Pope John Paul II issued an encyclical letter on the Eucharist entitled *Ecclesia de*

Eucharistia. In it, he directed the appropriate Roman Congregations to prepare and publish an Instruction, "including prescriptions of a juridical nature" that would explain the deeper meaning of liturgical norms in the light of liturgical abuses in violation of those same norms. *Sacrament of Redemption* is the response to that directive.

A booklet containing this document, "Instruction on the Eucharist," has been published by the United States Conference of Catholic Bishops Publishing (3211 Fourth Street NE, Washington DC, 20017; fax 202-722-8709; toll free 800-235-8722). Order No. 5-619. The booklet is 64 pages with the estimated price of $7.95.

Clergy and extraordinary ministers of Holy Communion will find its content inspirational, challenging, and informative. Many of the articles repeat norms contained in the *Roman Missal* and the pastoral *Introduction to the Order of Mass* that we already have included in this book. Nevertheless, there are additional points to be noted and we will treat some of them here.

OVERALL INNER ATTITUDES

Something more than mere external actions and proper observance of norms is necessary for the liturgy to fulfill its full and rich role in the Church. Article 5 of *Sacrament of Redemption* speaks to that point.

> The observance of the norms published by the authority of the Church requires conformity of thought and of word, of external action and of the application of the heart. A merely external observation of norms would obviously be contrary to the nature of the Sacred Liturgy, in which Christ himself wishes to gather his Church, so that together with himself she

will be "one body and one spirit." For this reason, external action must be illuminated by faith and charity, which unite us with Christ and with one another and engender love for the poor and the abandoned. The liturgical words and Rites, moreover, are a faithful expression, matured over the centuries, of the understanding of Christ, and they teach us to think as he himself does; by conforming our minds to these words, we raise our hearts to the Lord. All that is said in this Instruction is directed toward such a conformity of our own understanding with that of Christ, as expressed in the words and the Rites of the Liturgy.

Careful observance of liturgical norms promotes the unity of the Roman rite; careless neglect of them has the opposite effect. Article 11 addresses that issue:

The Mystery of the Eucharist "is too great for anyone to permit himself to treat it according to his own whim, so that its sacredness and its universal ordering would be obscured." On the contrary, anyone who acts thus by giving free reign to his own inclinations, even if he is a Priest, injures the substantial unity of the Roman Rite, which ought to be vigorously preserved, and becomes responsible for actions that are in no way consistent with the hunger and thirst for the living God that is experienced by the people today. Nor do such actions serve authentic pastoral care or proper liturgical renewal; instead, they deprive Christ's faithful of their patrimony and their heritage. For arbitrary actions are not conducive to true renewal, but are detrimental to the right of Christ's faithful to a liturgical celebration that is an expression of the Church's life in accordance with her tradition and discipline. In the end, they introduce elements of distortion and disharmony into the very celebration of the Eucharist, which is oriented in its own lofty way and by its very nature to signifying and wondrously bringing about the communion of divine life and the unity of the People of God. The result is uncertainty in matters of doctrine, perplexity and scandal on the part of the People of God, and, almost as a necessary consequence, vigorous opposition, all of which greatly confuse and sadden many of Christ's faithful in this age of ours when Christian life is often particularly difficult on account of the inroads of "secularization" as well.

EXTRAORDINARY MINISTERS

Chapter VII, "Extraordinary Functions of Lay Faithful" begins with eight articles treating this topic in a general way. Extraordinary ministers of Holy Communion will find these three of special interest:

146. There can be no substitute whatsoever for the ministerial Priesthood. For if a Priest is lacking in the community, then the community lacks the exercise and sacramental function of Christ the Head and Shepherd, which belongs to the essence of its very life. For "the only minister who can confect the sacrament of the Eucharist in *persona Christi* is a validly ordained Priest."

147. When the Church's needs require it, however, if sacred ministers are lacking, lay members of Christ's faithful may supply for certain liturgical offices according to the norm of law. Such faithful are called and appointed to carry out certain functions, whether of greater or lesser weight, sustained by the Lord's grace. Many of the lay Christian faithful have already contributed eagerly to this service and still do so, especially in missionary areas where the Church is still of small dimensions or is experiencing conditions

of persecution, but also in areas affected by a shortage of Priests and Deacons.

151. Only out of true necessity is there to be recourse to the assistance of extraordinary ministers in the celebration of the Liturgy. Such recourse is not intended for the sake of a fuller participation of the laity but rather, by its very nature, is supplementary and provisional. Furthermore, when recourse is had out of necessity to the functions of extraordinary ministers, special urgent prayers of intercession should be multiplied that the Lord may soon send a Priest for the service of the community and raise up an abundance of vocations to sacred Orders.

That chapter then dedicates a separate section (#1) to "The Extraordinary Minister of Holy Communion." These are the seven articles in it.

154. As has already been recalled, "the only minister who can confect the Sacrament of the Eucharist in *persona Christi* is a validly ordained Priest." Hence the name "minister of the Eucharist" belongs properly to the Priest alone. Moreover, also by reason of their sacred Ordination, the ordinary ministers of Holy Communion are the Bishop, the Priest and the Deacon, to whom it belongs therefore to administer Holy Communion to lay members of Christ's faithful during the celebration of Mass. In this way their ministerial Office in the Church is fully and accurately brought to light, and the sign value of the Sacrament is made complete.

155. In addition to the ordinary ministers there is the formally instituted acolyte, who by virtue of his institution is an extraordinary minister of Holy Communion even outside the celebration of Mass. If,

moreover, reasons of real necessity prompt it, another lay member of Christ's faithful may also be delegated by the diocesan Bishop, in accordance with the norm of law, for one occasion or for a specified time, and an appropriate formula of blessing may be used for the occasion. This act of appointment, however, does not necessarily take a liturgical form, nor, if it does take a liturgical form, should it resemble sacred Ordination in any way. Finally, in special cases of an unforeseen nature, permission can be given for a single occasion by the Priest who presides at the celebration of the Eucharist.

156. This function is to be understood strictly according to the name by which it is known, that is to say, that of extraordinary minister of Holy Communion, and not "special minister of Holy Communion" nor "extraordinary minister of the Eucharist" nor "special minister of the Eucharist," by which names the meaning of this function is unnecessarily and improperly broadened.

157. If there is usually present a sufficient number of sacred ministers for the distribution of Holy Communion, extraordinary ministers of Holy Communion may not be appointed. Indeed, in such circumstances, those who may have already been appointed to this ministry should not exercise it. The practice of those Priests is reprobated who, even though present at the celebration, abstain from distributing Communion and hand this function over to laypersons.

158. Indeed, the extraordinary minister of Holy Communion may administer Communion only when the Priest and Deacon are lacking, when the Priest is prevented by weakness or advanced age or some other genuine reason, or when the number of faithful

coming to Communion is so great that the very celebration of Mass would be unduly prolonged. This,
however, is to be understood in such a way that a brief
prolongation, considering the circumstances and culture of the place, is not at all a sufficient reason.

159. It is never allowed for the extraordinary minister
of Holy Communion to delegate anyone else to
administer the Eucharist, as for example a parent or
spouse or child of the sick person who is the communicant.

160. Let the diocesan Bishop give renewed consideration to the practice in recent years regarding this matter, and if circumstances call for it, let him correct it or
define it more precisely. Where such extraordinary
ministers are appointed in a widespread manner out
of true necessity, the diocesan Bishop should issue
special norms by which he determines the manner in
which this function is to be carried out in accordance
with the law, bearing in mind the tradition of the
Church.

A PARTICULAR CHANGE AND CLARIFICATION

Item 106 of this Instruction will necessitate a change
in the current process for distributing Holy Communion
under both kinds in many American parishes. It states:

106. However, the pouring of the Blood of Christ after
the consecration from one vessel to another is completely to be avoided, lest anything should happen
that would be to the detriment of so great a mystery.
Never to be used for containing the Blood of the Lord
are flagons, bowls, or other vessels that are not fully in
accord with the established norms.

That prohibition needs to be considered in relation to an earlier document approved on June 14, 2001, by the United States Conference of Catholic Bishops and subsequently confirmed by the Holy See in 2002. This document was titled *Norms for the Distribution and Reception of Holy Communion Under Both Kinds in the Dioceses of the United States of America.*

The following procedure, described in the March–April 2004 *Newsletter* of the USCCB's Secretariat for the Liturgy, harmonizes those two documents as well as the directives of the *Roman Missal* and the pastoral suggestions of the *Introduction to the Order of Mass.*

> The altar is prepared with corporal, purificator, Missal, and chalice (unless the chalice is prepared at a side table) by the deacon and servers. The gifts of bread and wine are brought forward by the faithful and received by the priest or deacon at a convenient place (Cf. GIRM, no. 333). (*Norms for the Distribution and Reception of Holy Communion Under Both Kinds in the Dioceses of the United States of America* (NDHC), no. 36)

> Because the instruction prohibits the consecration of wine in flagons, chalices for distribution to priests and to the faithful are prepared at this point. It should be noted that the principal chalice and the vessel containing the bread should be larger than the smaller vessels for distribution to the faithful. Smaller chalices of wine may be prepared at the altar or at a side table and are then suitably placed on the altar. "As the *Agnus Dei* or *Lamb of God* is begun, the Bishop or priest alone, or with the assistance of the deacon, and if necessary of concelebrating priests, breaks the eucharistic bread. Other empty...ciboria or patens are then brought to the altar if this is necessary. The dea-

con or priest places the consecrated bread in several ciboria or patens..., if necessary,...as required for the distribution of Holy Communion. If it is not possible to accomplish this distribution in a reasonable time, the celebrant may call upon the assistance of other deacons or concelebrating priests... (NDHC, no. 37)"

Notes

Chapter 1. The First Millennium and Early Middle Ages

1. Rev. Joseph A. Jungmann, SJ, *The Mass of the Roman Rite* (New York: Benziger Brothers, Inc., 1959), pp. 498–510.

2. *The Body of Christ,* Bishops' Committee on the Liturgy (Washington, DC: USCC Publications Office, 1977), pp. 11–15. This booklet, with its compilation of official documents on the Eucharist issued in recent years, includes an adaptation of an excellent historical overview of Communion in the hand by Archbishop Annibale Bugnini, then Secretary of the Congregation for Worship, which originally appeared in *L'Osservatore Romano* (English translation: *Origins,* August 15, 1973).

Chapter 2. A Contemporary Shift Backward and Forward

1. R. Kevin Seasoltz, *The New Liturgy: A Documentation 1903 to 1965* (New York: Herder and Herder, 1966). In the lengthy introduction, this Benedictine scholar presents a brief,

but thorough and interesting, historical overview of the contemporary liturgical movement. The text itself contains the salient official documents on the liturgy that have appeared during this period. My quotations from such decrees are generally excerpted from his volume.

2. Ibid., pp. xxvi–xxvii.

3. Ibid., p. 86.

4. Ibid., p. 91.

5. Ibid.

6. Ibid., p. 131.

7. Ibid., p. 478.

8. Ibid., p. 481.

9. Ibid.

10. *Study Text I, Holy Communion,* Bishops' Committee on the Liturgy (Washington, DC: United States Catholic Conference, 1979), pp. 3–10.

11. Ibid., p. 12.

12. This section of the Roman Ritual entitled *Holy Communion and Worship of the Eucharist Outside of Mass* has been divided into three distinct booklets published by the United States Catholic Conference, 13112 Massachusetts Avenue, NW, Washington, DC 20005: *Holy Communion Outside of Mass; Administration of Communion and Viaticum to the Sick by an Extraordinary Minister;* and *Forms of Worship of the Eucharist: Exposition, Benediction, Processions, Congresses.*

13. *Study Text I,* p. 3.

Chapter 3. Called to Holiness I:
Weak but Strong Persons of Faith

1. "Decree on the Ministry and Life of Priests," in *The Documents of Vatican II,* Walter M. Abbott, SJ, General Editor (New York: The America Press, 1966), article 12.

2. Matthew 26:40.

3. Matthew 26:41.

4. 2 Corinthians 12:8–10.

5. *Holy Communion Outside of Mass,* p. 4, article 6.

6. Ibid., p. 3, article 1.

7. Ibid., p. 3, article 2.

8. Ibid.

9. Ibid.

10. Luke 10:42.

11. *Music in Catholic Worship,* Bishops' Committee on the Liturgy (Washington, DC: United States Catholic Conference, 1983), p. 1, article 1.

12. Ibid., p. 1, article 4.

13. Ibid., p. 1, article 6.

14. Ibid., p. 4, article 21.

Chapter 4. Called to Holiness II:
Prayerful, Adoring, Joyful Ministers

1. Exodus 3:5–6.

2. *Holy Communion Outside of Mass,* p. 3, article 3.

3. *Forms of Worship of the Eucharist,* p. 7, articles 80–81.

4. *Holy Communion Outside of Mass,* p. 10, article 25.

5. Ibid.

6. *Selected Documentation from the Sacramentary* (Washington, DC: USCC Publications Office, 1974), p. 42, article 60. Also *General Instruction of the Roman Missal (Editio typical tertia),* Liturgy Documentary Series 2, United States Conference of Catholic Bishops (Washington, DC: USCC Publications Office, 2003), article 93.

7. Luke 2:10.

8. Luke 24:39–41.

9. Acts 2:46–47.

10. cf. Galatians 5:22–23.

11. 1 Thessalonians 5:16.

Chapter 5. Called to Holiness III:
Faith and Feelings, Laws and Life, Reverent but Relaxed

1. *Music in Catholic Worship*, p. 1, article 5.
2. *Holy Communion Outside of Mass*, pp. 9–10, article 23.
3. 1983 *Code of Canon Law*, Canon 919.
4. *Study Text I*, p. 15.
5. *Selected Documentation from the Sacramentary*, pp. 28–29, Chapter 1.
6. *Ibid*, pp. 40–41, articles 56, 56i.

Chapter 6. The Cup of Salvation

1. Matthew 26:26–28; see also Mark 14:22–25, Luke 22:14–20, 1 Corinthians 11:23 ff.
2. John 6:53.
3. *Norms for the Distribution and Reception of Holy Communion Under Both Kinds in the Dioceses of the United States of America*, Liturgy Documentary Series 13, United States Conference of Catholic Bishops (Washington, DC: USCCB Publishing, 2003), p. 9.
4. *The Body of Christ*, pp. 26–29. My historical treatment of Communion from the cup has been taken almost verbatim, with minor editing, from that text published by the Bishops' Committee on the Liturgy. The original booklet includes a half-dozen footnotes referring to official documents from which statements have been made or adapted.
5. *General Instruction of the Roman Missal (Editio typical tertia)*, article 281.
6. Matthew 26:29; see also Luke 22:18, Mark 14:25.
7. Eucharistic Prayer IV.
8. 1 Corinthians 10:16
9. Psalm 104:14–15.
10. Mark 10:38.
11. Matthew 27:42; see also Mark 14:32–42.
12. 1 Corinthians 10:21.

13. Eucharistic Prayer III.

14. Eucharistic Prayer IV.

15. Theodore of Mopsuestia, *Catechetical Homilies*, quoted in *Newsletter* from the Bishops' Committee on the Liturgy 14 (October 1978), pp. 135–36.

Chapter 7. Ministers of Mercy

1. *Communion of the Sick* (New Jersey: Catholic Book Publishing Co., 2000), pp. 5–6.

2. Ibid., pp. 46–47.

Chapter 8. Frequently Asked Questions I:
Theological Concerns

1. Romans 6:9.

Chapter 9. Frequently Asked Questions II:
Pastoral Issues

1. Alvin Toffler, *Future Shock* (New York: Random House, 1970), pp. 297–300.

2. John 15:5.

3. 2 Corinthians 12:1–10; quote is v. 9.

Chapter 10. Current Official Directives: *General Instruction of the Roman Missal*

1. The Bishops' Committee on the Liturgy, *Introduction to the Order of Mass*, Pastoral Liturgy Series 1 (Washington, DC: USCCB Publishing, 2003), p. xiii.
2. Ibid., p. xiv.

Chapter 11. A Pastoral Resource: *Introduction to the Order of Mass*

1. Introduction to the Order of Mass, p. xv.

Extraordinary Minister
of
Holy Communion
Certificate of Commissioning

⸎

This is to Certify

That _____

was commissioned an

Extraordinary Minister of
Holy Communion

according to the Rite of the Roman Catholic Church

on the_____ day of _____

in the year _____ at _____

Let us pray to God our Father that

_____,

chosen to administer the Body of Christ,
may be filled with His blessing.

⸎

_____

Dated

_____

Pastor